Women in
North America

DATE DUE

FE2 2'95			

DEMCO 38-297

Women in North America

Summaries of Biographical Articles in History Journals

People in History Series

Pamela R. Byrne and
Susan K. Kinnell, Editors

ABC·CLIO

Santa Barbara, California
Oxford, England

© 1988 by ABC-Clio, Inc.

Cover design by Tanya Nigh
Book design by Susan K. Kinnell

Library of Congress Cataloging in Publication Data

Women in North America.

 (The People in history series)
 Includes indexes.
 1. Women—United States—Biography. 2. Women—
Canada—Biography. 3. United States—Biography.
4. Canada—Biography. I. Byrne, Pamela R.
II. Kinnell, Susan K. III. Series.
CT3260.W664   1988   920.72'0971 88-6202
ISBN 0-87436-537-6 (pbk.)

10 9 8 7 6 5 4 3 2 1

ABC-Clio, Inc.
2040 Alameda Padre Serra, Box 4397
Santa Barbara, California 93103

Clio Press Ltd.
55 St. Thomas Street
Oxford, OX1 1JG, England

CONTENTS

PREFACE

This is a book about people — specifically, women in North America. Not every woman that you can think of is in this book, nor is every important thing mentioned about the women who are included. *WOMEN IN NORTH AMERICA* has 241 summaries of articles about US and Canadian women in all phases of their lives and work. There are as many unknown women here as there are famous ones — pioneer and frontier women, housewives, little-known poets, writers and musicians, actresses and photographers.

Using this volume, students can select topics for term papers and identify the names of specific women they wish to research further. Fictional or composite characters can be created by reading about several women doing the same kind of work or living in the same time and place. Role enactment in the classroom will be greatly enhanced by access to the people described in these summaries. Groups of women in history (such as the suffragettes) can be studied from several different perspectives, providing the teacher and the student with new approaches to learning.

WOMEN IN NORTH AMERICA differs from standard biographical dictionaries, which usually provide information about well-known people. Instead, this book brings to the reader's attention the lesser-known and the almost unknown women in American history in addition to a sampling of the famous ones. The chronological scope of the summaries ranges from the seventeenth century to the present, and the lives touched upon are those of women who have been the subjects of historians' research in the many journals covered in *America: History and Life*. The stories of these women will give a sense of the richness and diversity of everyday life at various times, providing a dimension to the study of history that is often missing in textbooks.

The entries in this book are summaries of some of the articles that have appeared over the years in thousands of history journals and that were selected by the editors at ABC-CLIO. It is to be hoped that the inclusion of varying sources (the journal literature from which these articles and summaries were taken) will direct students toward new avenues of research and help them consider new sources of information outside the realm of their usual classroom and library study. The list of journals covered in this book contains a number of titles that will be familiar to secondary school teachers and librarians and several that they may not previously have considered as a source for curriculum-based research. Interlibrary loans should provide access to these more unfamiliar journals so that further exploration and research may be carried out.

A NOTE ON HOW TO USE THIS BOOK:

The summaries are arranged alphabetically by the names of the women. A detailed subject index allows the student to find women by region, occupation, ethnic origin, or other unique factors. (See the note at the beginning of the index for a discussion on how to use this index.) All summaries and their original articles are in English. If there is more than one article about a particulr woman, the articles will appear alphabetically by the author of the article. If the original article had no author, the article is listed with the title first. A list of the article authors and the periodicals covered follows the subject index. A sample entry appears on the following page.

SAMPLE ENTRY

Name of Person

ALLEN, FLORENCE ELLINWOOD

Entry Number　　　Author

11. Cook, Beverly B.　THE FIRST WOMAN CANDIDATE FOR THE SUPREME COURT — FLORENCE E.ALLEN. *Supreme Court Hist. Soc. Y. 1981: 19-35.*

Article Title

Journal Information

Discusses the legal career of Florence Ellinwood Allen from 1914, when she received her law degree, to her death in 1966. During her career, Allen served most importantly as a member of the Ohio Supreme Court and as judge of the US Court of Appeals for the 6th Circuit. In the 1930's and 1940's, under Roosevelt and Truman, she was the first woman candidate for the US Supreme Court, largely due to the impetus supplied by the women's suffrage and reform movements. Explains the role of public opinion, politics, and the wishes of the sitting justices in her failure to be nominated.

Summary

WOMEN IN NORTH AMERICA

A

ADAMS, ABIGAIL

1. Cole, Adelaide M. ABIGAIL ADAMS: A VIGNETTE. *Daughters of the Am. Revolution Mag. 1979 113(5): 494-499.*

Abigail Adams (1744-1818) was the wife of John Adams, second president of the United States, and mother of John Quincy Adams. In 1840, her grandson, Charles Francis Adams, published two volumes of her letters.

2. Gelles, Edith B. ABIGAIL ADAMS: DOMESTICITY AND THE AMERICAN REVOLUTION. *New England Q. 1979 52(4): 500-521.*

Describes Abigail Adams's (1744-1818) management of the family farm and finances in Massachusetts. John Adams sent her tea, handkerchiefs, and other items from Europe. She sold or traded these to meet her needs and, during his absences, she invested in land. She fulfilled a man's role but was no feminist. "She believed that women were domestic, that their primary functions were within the home as wife and mother."

3. Palmer, Beverly Wilson. ABIGAIL ADAMS AND THE APPLE OF EUROPE. *New England Hist. and Geneal. Register 1981 135(Apr): 109-120.*

Abigail Adams's residence in England and France during 1784-88 is fully documented in her many letters to family and friends. They reveal how the experience changed her thinking about both the old world and the new. She recognized that she had idealized the new nation and that her hopes for a more virtuous government were probably unachievable.

ADAMS, LOUISA CATHERINE JOHNSON

4. Corbett, Katharine T. LOUISA CATHERINE ADAMS: THE ANGUISHED "ADVENTURES OF A NOBODY." Kelley, Mary, ed. *Woman's Being, Woman's Place: Female Identity and Vocation in American History (Boston: G. K. Hall, 1979): 67-84.*

Studies Louisa Catherine Adams, daughter-in-law of Abigail Adams. While Abigail personified Republican motherhood, Louisa, though fully committed to wifehood and motherhood, was unsuccessful in fulfilling the role. She considered herself an alien, possessing qualities of an upper-middle-class-English woman, which were inappropriate for the United States. Her relationship with her husband was strained, as was her relationship with her children. The interest in Louisa Adams lies not so much in the experience of failure as in her ability to articulate that experience. Her memoirs and letters for 1797-1812 shed light upon the role played by large numbers of women, the inherent strains in the role, and its effect upon the conception of self.

ADAMS, MARY NEWBURY

5. Lex, Louise Moede. MARY NEWBURY ADAMS: FEMINIST FORERUNNER FROM IOWA. *Ann. of Iowa 1976 43(5): 323-341.*

Through her writing, speaking, and organizational abilities, Iowan Mary Newbury Adams (1837-1901) tried to change the attitudes of 19th-century women toward themselves. Women, she believed, needed to know much more about their own history because knowledge of what women in the past had achieved would encourage succeeding generations. A forerunner in the struggle for female equality, Adams helped prepare the way for eventual improvement in the social status of women.

ADAMSON, SARAH BROWNE ARMSTRONG

6. Riley, Glenda and Benning, Carol. THE 1836-1845 DIARY OF SARAH BROWNE ARMSTRONG ADAMSON OF FAYETTE COUNTY, OHIO. *Old Northwest 1984 10(3): 285-306.*

Discusses the life of Sarah Browne Armstrong Adamson (1783-1851) and her diary, which gives a detailed account of her family's economic, social, and personal activities on their Fayette County, Ohio, farm. Selections from the diary, including poetry, offer insights into the primary interests and concerns of a farm woman and her family on the farm frontier in the mid-19th century.

ADDAMS, JANE

7. Barker-Benfield, G. J. MOTHER EMANCIPATOR: THE MEANING OF JANE ADDAMS' SICKNESS AND CURE. *J. of Family Hist. 1979 4(4): 395-420.*

Describes settlement house founder and social reformer Jane Addams's life as a struggle between "the values represented by her father and those she associated with her mother." Addams overtly rejected traditional maternal and wifely roles but found close psychological substitutes in her marriage to social reform and mothering of Hull House. Covers 1880-1920.

8. Cavallo, Dominick. SEXUAL POLITICS AND SOCIAL REFORM: JANE ADDAMS, FROM CHILDHOOD TO HULL HOUSE. Albin, Mel, ed. *New Directions in Psychohistory: The Adelphi Papers in Honor of Erik H. Erikson (Lexington, Mass.: Heath, 1980): 161-182.*

Studies social settlement worker Jane Addams's (1860-1935) childhood and adolescence, focusing on the cultural interfaces where individual life history meets social history and where biography and collective behavior interact. The problems and successes of Addams's early years were related to culturally prescribed paradigms of moral valuation and social behavior, especially the ways in which late-19th-century Americans perceived female and male social roles. The links between cultural paradigms and Addams's personal experiences, when placed in the context of late-19th-century urban and industrial changes, throw light on the relationship between her resolution of private conflicts and her decision to become a social reformer and thereby to help resolve society's public conflicts. She did this by opening Hull House, a social settlement institution, in Chicago in 1889.

ALCOTT, LOUISA MAY

9. Halttunen, Karen. THE DOMESTIC DRAMA OF LOUISA MAY ALCOTT. *Feminist Studies 1984 10(2): 233-254.*

The life and fiction of Louisa May Alcott are explored in the context of the influence of Bronson Alcott, Louisa's father, and changing Victorian society. Bronson Alcott, a transcendentalist, introduced theater to his young daughters in an effort to teach them purity of mind and body, and to establish a harmonious family and domestic bliss. Louisa May Alcott used theater to represent her personal struggle, as evidenced in the plays presented in *Little Women*, in which the March girls act out *Pilgrim's Progress* and "The Witch's Curse." In a larger context, Alcott's "domestic dramas" provide a mechanism by which the American Victorian family is preserved against the forces of Jacksonian individualism.

10. Stern, Madeleine B. LOUISA ALCOTT'S FEMINIST LETTERS. *Studies in the Am. Renaissance 1978: 429-452.*

Louisa May Alcott (1833-88) engaged in a variety of reform movements from abolitionism to temperance, but woman suffrage was her primary concern. In her correspondence, we can perceive her forceful commitment to feminism. Her activity was neither strident nor aggressive but rather "reflected the traditional values of her family. . . . Louisa Alcott's feminism of a human being impatient with indifference, apathy, and intolerance."

ALLEN, FLORENCE ELLINWOOD

11. Cook, Beverly B. THE FIRST WOMAN CANDIDATE FOR THE SUPREME COURT—FLORENCE E. ALLEN. *Supreme Court Hist. Soc. Y. 1981: 19-35.*

Discusses the legal career of Florence Ellinwood Allen from 1914, when she received her law degree, to her death in 1966. During her career, Allen served most importantly as a member of the Ohio Supreme Court and as judge of the US Court of Appeals for the 6th Circuit. In the 1930's and 1940's, under Roosevelt and Truman, she was the first woman candidate for the US Supreme Court, largely due to the impetus supplied by the women's suffrage and reform movements. Explains the role of public opinion, politics, and the wishes of the sitting justices in her failure to be nominated.

ALSTON, MARY NIVEN

12. Chitty, Arthur Ben. WOMEN AND BLACK EDUCATION: THREE PROFILES. *Hist. Mag. of the Protestant Episcopal Church 1983 52(2): 153-165.*

Brief vignettes of three women who made significant contributions to black higher education in the Protestant Episcopal Church. Anna Haywood Cooper (ca. 1858-1965) was only the fourth Negro woman to earn a doctorate from the Sorbonne—and at the age of 65. She became second president of Frelinghuysen University in Raleigh, North Carolina. While her forte was adult education, she never neglected the social and educational needs of children and youth. Isabella Gibson Robertson (1892-1976) was a financially comfortable white woman who was vitally concerned with supporting Saint Augustine College in Raleigh, North Carolina, a school she never saw but to which she contributed large sums. Mary Niven Alston (1918-81) was another white Episcopal woman who befriended black Episcopal schools. In her will she left $50,000 to Vorhees College in Denmark, South Carolina, a school she had never visited, but one of the numerous institutions she assisted in higher education.

AMES, MARY CLEMMER

13. Beasley, Maurine. MARY CLEMMER AMES: A
VICTORIAN WOMAN JOURNALIST.
Hayes Hist. J. 1978 2(1): 57-63.

Mary Clemmer Ames (1831-84) gained a national reputation as
a Washington correspondent through her column, "A Woman's
Letter From Washington," in the New York *Independent* (1866-
84). Her career illustrated how a woman could manipulate the
cultural framework of the Victorian period, and achieve success
without sacrificing her femininity. Though promoting the
Victorian ideology that women possessed purer morals than
men, Ames did not lead the kind of life her column advocated;
she was divorced and self-sufficient. It was Ames' womanly
duty, through her column, to campaign for an elevation of public
life.

ANCKER, HENRIETTA

14. Stern, Norton B. THE CHARITABLE JEWISH LADIES
OF SAN BERNARDINO AND THEIR WOMAN OF VALOR,
HENRIETTA ANCKER.
Western States Jewish Hist. Q. 1981 13(4): 369-376.

Henrietta Ancker (1835-90) came to San Bernardino, California,
with her husband Louis in 1870. She was very active in social
and charitable activities, and in 1886 she helped organize the
Ladies' Hebrew Benevolent Society. In tribute to her energetic
leadership, the members changed the name to the Henrietta
Hebrew Benevolent Society in 1891.

ANDERSON, MARGARET

15. Johnson, Abby Ann Arthur. THE PERSONAL
MAGAZINE: MARGARET C. ANDERSON AND THE
LITTLE REVIEW, 1914-1929.
South Atlantic Q. 1976 75(3): 351-363.

Margaret Anderson edited and controlled all the articles
appearing in the *Little Review*. The magazine reflected her

interests in feminism, world peace, literary censorship, and Dada art. Ezra Pound spent several years as foreign editor of the journal, getting the early works of Ford Madox Ford, T. S. Eliot, W. B. Yeats, and others, published for the first time in the United States. James Joyce's *Ulysses* appeared in serial form in 1918 and provoked a tremendous legal struggle. In 1923 Anderson turned control over to her lifelong companion Jane Heap, who kept the *Little Review* fitfully alive for only a few years.

ANDRADE, FLORES DE

16. Gamio, Manuel. SENORA FLORES DE ANDRADE. Mora, Magdalena and DelCastillo, Adelaida R., ed. *Mexican Women in the United States: Struggles Past and Present (Los Angeles: U. of California Chicano Studies Res. Center, 1980): 189-192.*

Provides a personal account of the life of Flores de Andrade, a Mexican immigrant who came to El Paso, Texas, in 1906. In 1909 she founded the Daughters of Cuauhtemoc, a women's secret organization allied with the Liberal Party in opposition to the dictatorship of Porfirio Diaz in Mexico. In 1911 she was nearly executed for her activities, but escaped. Reprinted from Manuel Gamio's *The Mexican Immigrant: His Life Story* (1931).

ANTHONY, SUSAN B.

17. Beeton, Beverly and Edwards, G. Thomas. SUSAN B. ANTHONY'S WOMAN SUFFRAGE CRUSADE IN THE AMERICAN WEST. *J. of the West 1982 21(2): 5-15.*

In 1871 Susan B. Anthony and Elizabeth Cady Stanton visited several western states. They were especially interested in Wyoming and Utah where women had equal suffrage, but spoke everywhere they traveled on issues important in the women's movement. While Mrs. Stanton's talks had some favorable press reviews, their feminist causes were denounced by the opinion makers—the politicians, ministers, and editors. Anthony returned to the West in 1877, 1895, and 1896. By the time of her last trip, at age 76, Anthony's views had gained popularity and respect. Women's rights leaders concentrated on the single issue of suffrage and went directly to the opinion makers to educate them and to persuade them to support the goal of suffrage.

ANTISARLOOK, MARY

18. Ray, Dorothy Jean. SINROCK MARY: FROM ESKIMO WIFE TO REINDEER QUEEN. *Pacific Northwest Quarterly 1984 75(3): 98-107.*

Sheldon Jackson, Presbyterian missionary and first general agent of education for Alaska, imported a domesticated reindeer herd from Russia to Alaska in 1892 to provide a new industry for Eskimos. He initiated the experiment on the Sinuk River and placed the herd under the supervision of Charlie and Mary Antisarlook. Under their careful management the herd increased, but Charlie's death in 1900 sparked a legal battle with his relatives who wished to take control of the herd from Mary. Her courtroom victory was expensive, but Mary emerged with full control of the reindeer. Prior to her death in 1948, Mary had become a legend because of her generosity toward other Eskimos and her adoption of eleven Eskimo children.

ARMER, LAURA ADAMS

19. Dicker, Laverne Mau. LAURA ADAMS ARMER, CALIFORNIA PHOTOGRAPHER. *California Hist. Q. 1977 56(2): 128-139.*

Laura Adams Armer (1874-1963), a native Californian, achieved fame as a portrait photographer, artist, author, film producer, and historian. After studying painting and drawing she took up photography in 1899, favoring the new concept of naturalistic photography. Her photographs were notable for the use of light and shadow and lack of contrivance. In 1902 she married Sidney Armer and gave up her career for the next 20 years. She recommenced her career at age 50 and developed an interest in Indians' folklore, particularly Navajo and Hopi sandpainting. She produced an Indian-language motion picture in 1928 and went on to write and illustrate children's books and essays on Indian culture.

ATHERTON, GERTRUDE

20. Forrey, Carolyn. GERTRUDE ATHERTON AND THE NEW WOMAN. *California Hist. Q. 1976 55(3): 194-209.*

Describes the career of Gertrude Atherton (1857-1948), author of 56 novels and numerous stories. Strongwilled and rebellious in her youth, Atherton found an intellectual outlet in writing fiction. Following the early death of her husband in a loveless marriage, Atherton set out to pursue a literary career. After initial unfavorable reviews she went to Europe and became a huge success there, particularly in England. A favorable reception to her novels then followed in the United States. The heroines in Atherton's novels fit the pattern of the "New Woman"—intellectually superior, athletic, independent, and sexually attractive. Such heroines greatly resembled Atherton's self-image. She had no patience with men who stereotyped women as submissive home-bound objects lacking intellectual capacity. Moreover, her heroines, in combining intellect with sexuality, represented a definition of feminism that Atherton herself attempted to fulfill throughout her long life.

B

BARA, THEDA

21. Lockwood, Charles. PRIESTESS OF SIN. *Horizon 1981 24(1): 64-69.*

Theda Bara, who acted the vamp both on and off screen from 1915 to 1919, served as an ideal sex symbol in that she offered sexual allure without seriously threatening the morality of the time.

BARNEY, NATALIE CLIFFORD

22. Orenstein, Gloria Feman. THE SALON OF NATALIE CLIFFORD BARNEY: AN INTERVIEW WITH BERTHE CLEYRERGUE. *Signs 1979 4(3): 484-496.*

Describes the activities and life-style of American writer Natalie Clifford Barney, through an interview with her French companion and servant of 45 years, Berthe Cleyrergue. Barney maintained a legendary salon in Paris from 1909 until her death in 1972, where frequent visitors included Gertrude Stein, Alice B. Toklas, Romaine Brooks, and Dolly Wilde. Suggests the need for further research on the history of female support networks like the one fostered by Barney.

BARTON, CLARA

23. Gilbo, Patrick F. CANDID, "CRANKY" CLARA BARTON GAVE US THE RED CROSS.
Smithsonian 1981 12(2): 126-142.

Recounts the sometimes stormy career of Clara Barton, the founder of the American Red Cross, who led the organization from its founding in 1881 to 1904 and who conducted 19 major relief operations.

24. Henle, Ellen Langenheim. CLARA BARTON, SOLDIER OR PACIFIST?
Civil War Hist. 1978 24(2): 152-160.

The study of Clara Barton, founder of the American Red Cross and active in three major wars, contributes new perspectives on women's future military roles. She viewed war as a fact of life and wanted women to take part in it, including military education and combat service. She believed that women's secondary citizen status was directly related to exclusion from war. A complex person, Clara Barton was attracted and repelled by war. She viewed herself as a soldier, appreciating the adventure; in a real sense, her humanitarianism provided an alternative to a military career. Yet she genuinely longed for and worked for peace, particularly through her Red Cross movement.

25. Stewart, Sally. SHARING MORE THAN MARBLE PALACES.
Daughters of the Am. Revolution Mag. 1981 115(3): 188-191.

Clara Barton, Mabel Boardman, and Jane Delano were all both Daughters of the American Revolution and American Red Cross pioneers: Clara Barton served as a Civil War nurse and founded the American Red Cross in 1881; Mabel Boardman served as a Red Cross administrator for four decades until 1944; and Jane Delano, as head of the National Committee on Red Cross Nursing Service, administered the Red Cross nursing operation during World War I.

BATES, DAISY

26. Trescott, Jacqueline. DAISY BATES: BEFORE AND AFTER LITTLE ROCK. *Crisis 1981 88(5): 232-235.*

Daisy Bates, a journalist and civil rights leader, was an important worker behind the scene during the armed crisis surrounding the integration of Central High School in Little Rock, Arkansas, in 1957. As founder and editor of the *Arkansas State Press* and leader of the state's NAACP, she had been a crusader against discrimination from the 1940's. Bates prepared the children and community for the 1957 struggle. She built bridges between both sides as the conflict raged. Her home became the target of fire bombs, rocks, gun fire, and burning crosses. Quietly, she negotiated a solution.

BEALS, JESSIE TARBOX

27. Moenster, Kathleen. JESSIE BEALS: OFFICIAL PHOTOGRAPHER OF THE 1904 WORLD'S FAIR. *Gateway Heritage 1982 3(2): 22-29.*

Jessie Tarbox Beals (1870-1942) defied tradition to become the first woman photographer officially accredited to photograph the 1904 Louisiana Purchase Exposition at St. Louis, Missouri. Her success in 1904 led to a professional career in photography. She ventured abroad, performing overseas assignments in Latin America, Africa, and Asia. Beals published extensively in American newspapers and magazines, and her fame ensured her a place on the public lecture circuit.

BEARD, MARY RITTER

28. Smith, Bonnie G. SEEING MARY BEARD. *Feminist Studies 1984 10(3): 399-416.*

Reviews Mary Beard's historiography, using the viewpoint she herself applied to history. Just as she noted that women are invisible to historians, her work has been largely ignored or misunderstood by others. She rejected the accumulation of facts as a tool for understanding history. Crucial to understanding Mary Beard's "weirdness and asymmetry" is a recognition of her belief in history as viewpoint, and that the absence or presence of women in history depends entirely on the perspective of the historian. The fact that she did not receive full recognition for her work, whereas her husband Charles Beard was given both blame and credit for it, reinforces her own observations about history and historians.

BECK, MARY MENESSIER

29. Whitley, Edna Talbot. MARY BECK AND THE FEMALE MIND. *Register of the Kentucky Hist. Soc. 1979 77(1): 15-24.*

Mary Menessier Beck was born in France and came to the United States with her husband, artist George Beck, sometime during 1792-99. In 1805, Beck opened an academy for girls in Lexington, Kentucky. With a full curriculum, Beck broke with the tradition that suggested less education for women. Among her students during her nearly 35 years of educating young women was Mary Todd.

BEECHER, CATHERINE

30. Lambert, Pierre D. WOMEN IN EDUCATION: THE KNOWN, THE FORGOTTEN, THE UNKNOWN. *Vitae Scholasticae 1983 2(1): 93-112.*

Presents biographical sketches of seven American women educators: Emma Willard, who supported women's education in New England and New York; Mary Lyon, who founded Mount

Holyoke Seminary in 1837; Catherine Beecher, who started women's schools in Hartford and Cincinnati; Helen Parkhurst, who studied under Maria Montessori in Italy and promoted her system of education in the United States, devising the Dalton Plan of individualized contracts for students; Caroline Pratt, who founded the City and Country School in Greenwich Village in 1914; and Lucy Sprague Mitchell and Marietta Johnson, both of whom were progressive educators.

BEESON, DESDEMONA STOTT

31. James, Laurence P. and Taylor, Sandra C. "STRONG MINDED WOMEN": DESDEMONA STOTT BEESON AND OTHER HARD ROCK MINING ENTREPRENEURS. *Utah Hist. Q. 1978 46(2): 136-150.*

Desdemona Stott Beeson (1897-1976), trailblazer for women in mining, grew up in a Utah mining camp. She married geologist Joseph J. Beeson, took courses in mining engineering and geology, and was her husband's partner as an independent mining entrepreneur. Other women in the early 20th century whose knowledge of mining engineering or ability to handle financial operations gained them status as "female mining men" were Leatha Millard Arnott, Lena Larsen, Mrs. Mary J. Stewart, Elizabeth Pollet, and Josie Pearl.

BENEDICT, RUTH FULTON

32. Briscoe, Virginia Wolf. RUTH BENEDICT: ANTHROPOLOGICAL FOLKLORIST. *J. of Am. Folklore 1979 92(366): 445-476.*

Ruth Benedict's (1887-1948) work as an anthropological folklorist centered on the themes of cultural configuration and cultural relativism. She encouraged great activity by women in the American Folklore Society during the 1920's and 1930's, and became recognized as a founder of the Culture and Personality school of anthropology.

BERRY, MARTHA

33. Henry, Inez. FAMOUS GEORGIA WOMEN: MARTHA BERRY. *Georgia Life 1979 6(2): 30-32.*

Martha Berry (1866-1942) of Oak Hill, Georgia, founded four Sunday schools, four day schools, the Boy's Industrial School (changed in 1909 to the Berry Schools, with the addition of a girl's school), and a Junior College.

BERTINATTI, EUGENIA BATE BASS

34. Durham, Walter T. TENNESSEE COUNTESS. *Tennessee Hist. Q. 1980 39(3): 323-340.*

Tennessee-born Eugenia Bate Bass (1826-1906), widow of a wealthy Mississippi planter, dazzled Washington society in 1865 by marrying Count Giuseppe Bertinatti, the Italian envoy. She traveled between the United States and Italy, visiting frequently her family in Tennessee, while watching over her estates, especially Riverside Plantation in Mississippi. She eventually settled in Nashville, where she died.

BETHUNE, JOANNA GRAHAM

35. Miller, Page Putnam. WOMEN IN THE VANGUARD OF THE SUNDAY SCHOOL MOVEMENT. *J. of Presbyterian Hist. 1980 58(4): 311-325.*

Examines the leadership of three Presbyterian women in the Sunday school movement: Joanna Graham Bethune (1770-1860), who organized a school in New York's Brick Presbyterian Church, which ultimately led to a full-grown Sunday school; Margaretta Mason Brown (1772-1838), who organized the first Sunday school in Kentucky, out of which was formed the First Presbyterian Church of Frankfort; and Anne Clay (1796-1844), who organized a Sabbath School on her brother's plantation in Georgia for the instruction of slave children. The Sunday school movement opened up a whole array of opportunities for women, not only providing them the opportunity for classroom teaching, but also the potential for social work, theological study, preparation of curriculum materials, establishment of libraries, innovation of teaching methods, organization of local schools, and experience in a national institutional network.

BEVIER, ISABEL

36. Bartow, Beverly. ISABEL BEVIER AT THE UNIVERSITY OF ILLINOIS AND THE HOME ECONOMICS MOVEMENT. *J. of the Illinois State Hist. Soc. 1979 72(1): 21-38.*

Reviews the life and works of Isabel Bevier (1860-1942), especially in relation to her pioneer work in home economics at the University of Illinois during 1900-21. Covers briefly the first halting steps in the field, beginning with the acceptance of women in universities. Bevier came to the University of Illinois from a solid educational background, determined to place home management on the level of a science. Relates the steps she took to do so, the victories, and the trials and tribulations. Closes with a few notes about her later works.

BIDAMON, EMMA HALE SMITH

37. Avery, Valeen Tippetts and Newell, Linda King. THE LION AND THE LADY: BRIGHAM YOUNG AND EMMA SMITH. *Utah Hist. Q. 1980 48(1): 81-97.*

After Joseph Smith's death in 1844, Emma Hale Smith (later Bidamon) and Brigham Young conflicted over the succession to the Mormons' presidency, and the settling of Joseph's estate. Young felt that Emma had taken property belonging to the Mormons. Emma's legacy of debt left her feeling that Young had swindled her out of wealth. Neither understood that there had been no wealth. Nauvoo, Illinois, was built on speculative economy. Their conflict led to later institutionalized rancor between two churches (the Latter-day Saints and the Reorganized Latter-day Saints) claiming the same founder.

38. Avery, Valeen Tippetts. EMMA SMITH THROUGH HER WRITINGS.
Dialogue 1984 17(3): 101-106.

Surveys the letters of Emma Hale Smith Bidamon (1804-79) for evidence of the woman as she understood herself. She was Joseph Smith's faithful and loving wife, as can be seen from his letters to her, including one written on the day he was murdered, 27 June 1844. Many Mormons resented her subsequent marriage to Lewis Bidamon and her refusal to follow Brigham Young to Utah. While members of the (Utah) Church of Jesus Christ of Latter-Day Saints came to see her as an example of faithless perfidy, the (Missouri) Reorganized Church of Jesus Christ of Latter Day Saints regarded her as the embodiment of righteousness and the mother of their hereditary patriarchs.

39. Newell, Linda King. THE EMMA SMITH LORE RECONSIDERED.
Dialogue 1984 17(3): 86-100.

Controversy among Mormons about the wife of Joseph Smith, Emma Hale Smith Bidamon (1804-79), including semilegendary accounts that she burned his revelation on plural marriage, attempted to poison him, and was partly responsible for his death, arises from bitterness about her refusal to follow Brigham Young to Utah and her endorsement of her children's Reorganized Church of Jesus Christ of Latter Day Saints.

BIDWELL, ANNIE ELLICOTT KENNEDY

40. Mathes, Valerie Sherer. INDIAN PHILANTHROPY IN CALIFORNIA: ANNIE BIDWELL AND THE MECHOOPDA INDIANS.
Arizona and the West 1983 25(2): 153-166.

Using her own family resources and acting on her own initiative, Annie Ellicott Kennedy Bidwell worked with a small band of California Mechoopda Indians to "civilize" them. Encouragd by her wealthy California rancher and congressman husband, she worked closely with the Mechoopda, provided them a school and a church, and supported them financially almost from her marriage in 1868 to her death.

BISHOP, HARRIET E.

41. Bolin, Winifred D. Wandersee. HARRIET E. BISHOP: MORALIST AND REFORMER. Stuhler, Barbara and Kreuter, Gretchen, ed. *Women of Minnesota: Selected Biographical Essays (St. Paul:Minnesota Historical Society Press, 1977): 7-19.*

In 1847, Harriet E. Bishop arrived in the frontier community of St. Paul, Minnesota. Trained by Catharine Beecher, Bishop brought with her the missionary zeal of the social reformer and a belief in the moral superiority of women. A Baptist, she established the first public school and the first Sunday School in St. Paul. Discusses her activities as a temperance advocate, largely negative attitudes toward the local Indians, efforts to help the destitute, prose and poetry, and two matrimonial opportunities. Bishop died in 1883. By then she was largely unknown in the growing metropolis, but her life "personified a whole generation of women" who tried to fulfill their destinies within the boundaries of convention and who labored to meet the responsibilities imposed by their presumed innate superiority.

BLAINE, ANITA MCCORMICK

42. Antler, Joyce. FEMALE PHILANTHROPY AND PROGRESSIVISM IN CHICAGO. *Hist. of Educ. Q. 1981 21(4): 461-469.*

Reviews Gilbert Harrison's *A Timeless Affair: The Life of Anita McCormick Blaine.* Blaine, born in 1876 to a wealthy Chicago family, was more than heiress to the McCormick reaper fortune. Impressed by the ideas of John Dewey and desirous of a good education for her son, she played an important part in developing progressive educational programs during the early 1900's. She also participated in world peace movements from World War I to the 1950's. Although not formally a feminist, she was peripherally engaged in the suffrage struggle through work with such groups as Hull House, the Women's Trade Union League, and the Consumer's League. Her life exemplified the influence of women on philanthropic and progressive trends, but also revealed conflicts faced by career-oriented women.

BLAIR, ELIZABETH

43. Laas, Virginia J. THE COURTSHIP AND MARRIAGE OF ELIZABETH BLAIR AND SAMUEL PHILLIPS LEE: A PROBLEM IN HISTORICAL DETECTION. *Midwest Quarterly 1985 27(1): 13-29.*

The four-year courtship of Elizabeth Blair and Samuel Phillips Lee illustrates the complexities of social customs among antebellum America's middle and upper classes. Blair, part of a powerful Washington political family, and Lee, a career navy officer and grandson of Richard Henry Lee, had to deal with the separations caused by navy life and the disapproval of Elizabeth's father, partly due to Samuel's position in society. The two left a trail of correspondence that enables historians to piece together their tumultuous courtship and wedding and thus understand the formation of an important political and military couple.

BLAKE, ALICE

44. Foote, Cheryl J. ALICE BLAKE OF TREMENTINA: MISSION TEACHER OF THE SOUTHWEST. *J. of Presbyterian Hist. 1982 60(3): 228-242.*

Alice Blake was typical of devout American Presbyterian women who felt the call to take the civilizing aspects of the Protestant gospel to those who were under the iron hand of Romanism in the Southwest. Chronicles her labors, which culminated in the village of Trementina, New Mexico, where she labored for 30 years. In addition to being a teacher, she took the necessary courses that qualified her as a public health nurse, while at the same time she filled in from time to time as leader in worship when no minister was present. Protestant mission teachers like Blake came to the area laden with the same attitudes of ethnic and cultural superiority that characterized their countrymen. But they also brought a firm and sincere commitment to the Christian faith and a loving desire to serve.

BLALOCK, ALICE GRUNDY

45. Carter, Doris Dorcas. ALICE GRUNDY BLALOCK: A PORTRAIT OF LOVE. *North Louisiana Hist. Assoc. J. 1982 13(4): 131-138.*

Alice Grundy Blalock was a leader in the struggle to eliminate illiteracy in the black communities of Louisiana. Prior to beginning her long career as a teacher-trainer at Louisiana Normal and Industrial Institute (now Grambling State University) in 1929, she taught successfully in several public schools. She worked hard to make Grambling a reputable institution of higher learning and earned a reputation as a "master teacher."

BLOOMER, AMELIA JENKS

46. Noun, Louise. AMELIA BLOOMER, A BIOGRAPHY: PART I, THE LILY OF SENECA FALLS. *Annals of Iowa 1985 47(7): 575-617.*

Born and reared in New York, Amelia Jenks Bloomer worked during most of her early life as a temperance leader. Married to Dexter Bloomer, she continued her temperance activities, writing newspaper articles. During this time she joined the suffragette movement, and her newspaper, the *Lily*, became the principal outlet for her views after 1850. Bloomer pioneered a change in women's clothing, although she was mocked for wearing the infamous pants named for her. With Elizabeth Cady Stanton she campaigned for women's suffrage, and in 1854, she moved to Council Bluffs, Iowa, continuing publication of the *Lily* there.

BONNIN,GERTRUDE SIMMONS (ZITKALA SA)

47. Fisher, Dexter. ZITKALA SA: THE EVOLUTION OF A WRITER. *Am. Indian Q. 1979 5(3): 229-238.*

Gertrude Simmons Bonnin (Zitkala Sa), a Yankton Sioux, left home at eight to study in boarding school and later attended

Earlham College. Adopting the name Zitkala Sa, she won writing honors before marrying and beginning work for Indian citizenship, employment, and land claims. She founded the National Council of American Indians in 1926 and served as president until her death in 1938. She had found a way to use her white-taught communication skills on behalf of Indians.

BORG, SELMA JOSEFINA

48. Myhrman, Anders. SELMA JOSEFINA BORG: FINLAND: SWEDISH MUSICIAN, LECTURER, AND CHAMPION OF WOMEN'S RIGHTS. *Swedish Pioneer Hist. Q. 1979 30(1): 25-34.*

Selma Josefina Borg was born in Gamlarkarleby, Finland, in 1838, the youngest of nine children in an apparently well-to-do middle-class family. She studied music in Finland, Sweden, and Switzerland. She taught music in Helsinki for some years before coming in 1864 to Philadelphia, where she established herself as a private music and language teacher. In collaboration with Marie A. Brown, she began translating current Swedish works into English. Borg joined a women's committee formed to promote the Centennial Exposition of 1876 in Philadelphia and returned to Finland in 1875 to arouse interest and possibly participation in the celebration. She had, by this time, become a champion of the rights of women and most of her lectures dealt with developments and conditions in America. Describes her lecture tour. Returning to America, she became well known as a musician and speaker on women's rights.

BOSQUE Y FANQUI, CAYETANA SUSANA

49. DeGrummond, Jane Lucas. CAYETANA SUSANA BOSQUE Y FANQUI, "A NOTABLE WOMAN." *Louisiana Hist. 1982 23(3): 277-294.*

Life of a noted New Orleans beauty, the second wife of the provisional governor of Louisiana and later US Senator William Charles Cole Claiborne and, after his death, wife of John R. Grymes, lawyer and former US district attorney for the Louisiana district. Includes information on the careers of her husbands and the marital adventures of her numerous offspring.

BOWER, BERTHA MUZZY

50. Bloodworth, William A., Jr. MULFORD AND BOWER: MYTH AND HISTORY IN THE EARLY WESTERN. *Great Plains Q. 1981 1(2): 95-104.*

Discusses the western novels of Clarence Edward Mulford, who created Hopalong Cassidy, and Bertha Muzzy Bower, the only woman to become an important writer of westerns, comparing their westerns as sources of comedy and their emphasis on themes of community rather than individualism as reflective of the optimism of the Progressive Era; 1904-16.

BOYD, BELLE

51. Davis, Curtis Carroll. "THE PET OF THE CONFEDERACY" STILL? FRESH FINDINGS ABOUT BELLE BOYD. *Maryland Hist. Mag. 1983 78(1): 35-53.*

Recounts the life of Belle Boyd, who during the Civil War achieved notoriety as a spy for the Confederacy. Boyd suffered two failed marriages and bouts with insanity after the war. She eventually formed a theatrical group with her third husband and travelled through the country presenting reenactments of wartime events.

BOYD, HELEN

52. Boyd, Helen; Crawley, T. A., ed. GROWING UP PRIVILEGED IN EDMONTON. *Alberta Hist. (Canada) 1982 30(1): 1-10.*

Daughter of a prominent Albertan politician, Helen Boyd (1905-80) reminisces about her early childhood in Edmonton. Notes such matters as tent-dwellers, family attempts at gardening, impact of the outbreak of World War I, her early schooling, fear of diseases, and summer vacations in the country. Refers to such leading politicians as Clifford Sifton, especially with reference to social events.

BRADFORD, CORNELIA

53. Handen, Ella. IN LIBERTY'S SHADOW: CORNELIA
BRADFORD AND WHITTIER HOUSE.
New Jersey History 1982 100(3-4): 48-69.

During the 1890's, Cornelia Bradford, the fairly well-to-do
daughter of a Congregationalist minister, established Whittier
House as the first settlement house in Jersey City, New Jersey.
Influenced by activities of English settlement houses, Bradford
hoped to provide services to city residents that their government
could not. A kindergarten, dispensary, and summer youth camp
were three of her programs. In addition to reform interests
locally, Bradford involved herself in statewide efforts. She
retired in 1926 and by the time of her death had witnessed her
settlement house change into a boy's club.

BRADLEY, MARY

54. Bradley, Mary. MARY BRADLEY'S
REMINISCENCES: A DOMESTIC LIFE IN COLONIAL
NEW BRUNSWICK.
Atlantis (Canada) 1981 7(1): 92-101.

Born in Gagetown, New Brunswick, in 1771, Mary Bradley (nee
Coy) "experienced religion" at age 16. Kept from public
speaking by conventions of the time Bradley married in 1793
and sought fulfillment through marriage. Unsuccessful in this
attempt she eventually joined the Methodist Church whose
"doctrines best reflected her own well-thought-out religious
views and which offered an expanding sphere for female
energy."

BRADSTREET, ANNE

55. King, Anne. ANNE HUTCHINSON AND ANNE
BRADSTREET: LITERATURE AND EXPERIENCE, FAITH
AND WORKS IN MASSACHUSETTS BAY COLONY.
Int. J. of Women's Studies (Canada) 1978 1(5): 445-467.

Examines the lives and political, religious, and social attitudes of Anne Hutchinson (1591-1643) and Anne Bradstreet (1612-72) who, through polarizing the question of faith versus works and through questioning the position of women, introduced tensions in American life and ideology which led to eventual social change.

BRANSTEN, FLORINE HAAS

56. Dalin, David G. FLORINE AND ALICE HAAS AND THEIR FAMILIES. *Western States Jewish Hist. Q. 1981 13(2): 135-141.*

Florine Haas Bransten (1881-1973) and Alice Haas Lilienthal (1885-1972), daughters of San Francisco merchant William Haas, were leaders of the city's social and cultural community as their husbands were prominent in business. The Haas-Lilienthal House on Franklin Street, commissioned by William Haas in 1886, and inherited by Alice, is a San Francisco historical landmark.

BRECKINRIDGE, MARY

57. Campbell, Anne G. MARY BRECKINRIDGE AND THE AMERICAN COMMITTEE FOR DEVASTATED FRANCE: THE FOUNDATIONS OF THE FRONTIER NURSING SERVICE. *Register of the Kentucky Hist. Soc. 1984 82(3): 257-276.*

Mary Breckinridge established the Frontier Nursing Service in Leslie County, Kentucky, in 1925. Building on her two years of experience with a relief agency in post-World War I France, she established a headquarters and centers around outlying areas, bringing medical treatment to remote areas. World War I thus contributed to improved medical services in rural Appalachia.

58. Crowe-Carraco, Carol. MARY BRECKINRIDGE AND THE FRONTIER NURSING SERVICE. *Register of the Kentucky Hist. Soc. 1978 76(3): 179-191.*

Personal tragedies led Mary Breckinridge to work for a family centered health care system in frontier Kentucky areas. From the mid-1920's until her death 40 years later, Breckinridge and the Frontier Nursing Service provided assistance in midwifery, general family care, and disease prevention. From small beginnings, the FNS network grew to cover an area of almost 700 square miles.

59. Dye, Nancy Schrom. MARY BRECKINRIDGE, THE FRONTIER NURSING SERVICE AND THE INTRODUCTION OF NURSE-MIDWIFERY IN THE UNITED STATES. *Bulletin of the Hist. of Medicine 1983 57(4): 485-507.*

In 1925, Mary Breckinridge, a trained nurse, established the Frontier Nursing Service (FNS) in an attempt to transplant the European tradition of professional midwifery to the United States. She not only reduced infant and maternal mortality in a rural county in the heart of Appalachia, but she pioneered in developing an autonomous professional role for nurses and established the profession of nurse-midwifery in the United States. Her work spread to other counties in Kentucky, but she was unable to secure funding to expand into other areas, a situation exacerbated by the Depression. Breckinridge never intended that the FNS should challenge the medical system directly, but envisioned a program for impoverished rural areas lacking physicians.

60. Matthies, Katharine. MARY BRECKINRIDGE AND THE FRONTIER NURSING SERVICE. *Daughters of the Am. Revolution Mag. 1980 114(5): 692-694.*

Mary Breckinridge (1889-1965) served in Washington, D.C., during the influenza epidemic in 1918, was a volunteer for the American Committee for Devastated France during 1918-20, became a certified midwife serving rural Kentucky mountaineers, and established the Frontier Nursing Service.

BRECKINRIDGE, SOPHINISBA P.

61. Travis, Anthony R. SOPHINISBA BRECKINRIDGE, MILITANT FEMINIST. *Mid-America 1976 58(2): 111-118.*

Sophinisba Breckinridge, 1866-1948, was a militant suffragette, progressive reformer, women's rights advocate, the first woman-appointee to the Kentucky bar, trade-union advocate, author of numerous works on urban-industrial problems, and professor of public welfare at the University of Chicago. Concerned for professional and working-class women as well as for prostitutes, she opposed the Equal Rights Amendment because of its possible effect on protective legislation for working women. She was influenced by Hull House and devoted her life to generous and public-spirited effort.

BREEDEN, JANE ROOKER SMITH

62. Otto, Kathryn. DAKOTA RESOURCES: THE JANE BREEDEN PAPERS AT THE SOUTH DAKOTA HISTORICAL RESOURCE CENTER. *South Dakota Hist. 1980 10(3): 241-244.*

Jane Rooker Smith Breeden (1853-1955) was a leader of the woman suffrage and temperance movements in South Dakota. Along with material on the suffrage and temperance activities, the papers include items about other social organizations with which Breeden was involved, and information on World War I anti-German propaganda.

BRIN, FANNY FLIGELMAN

63. Stuhler, Barbara. FANNY BRIN: WOMAN OF PEACE. Stuhler, Barbara and Kreuter, Gretchen, ed. *Women of Minnesota: Selected Biographical Essays (St. Paul: Minnesota Historical Society Press, 1977): 284-300.*

In 1884, three-month-old Fanny Fligelman came to Minneapolis with her Romanian Jewish parents. A serious student in high school and at the University of Minnesota, Fanny was active in the Minerva Literature Society and was elected to Phi Beta Kappa. She became a teacher, and in 1913 wed Arthur Brin, a successful businessman. Fanny raised a family, became a prominent volunteer activist, and worked for woman suffrage, world peace, democracy, and Jewish heritage. During the 1920's and 30's, she was especially active in the National Council of Jewish Women and served as director of the Minneapolis Woman's Committee for World Disarmament. Stimulated by the Nazi attack on Jews, Fanny became a strong Zionist. As the alternate delegate for the Women's Action Committee for Lasting Peace, Fanny attended the 1945 San Francisco meetings which gave birth to the United Nations. An excellent speaker, Fanny served in many organizations, promoted many causes, took civic responsibilities as serious duties, and worked to better use women and their contributions to improve world affairs.

BRINDLEY, ETHEL MAE

64. Brindley, Esther E. ETHEL MAE BRINDLEY, BIOGRAPHICAL SKETCH. *Chronicles of Oklahoma 1981 59(2): 237-240.*

Life on a turn of the century farm near Mustang, Oklahoma, proved hard but adventurous for Ethel Mae Brindley. The death of her husband in 1921 left Brindley without an income and she moved to Edmond, Oklahoma, to open a rooming house. During the 1920's she undertook several business ventures, including a very successful role as one of Oklahoma's first women oil brokers. Always civic-minded and progressive, she still remains active in Mustang's community affairs.

BRISCOE, ANNE M.

65. Briscoe, Anne M. DIARY OF A MAD FEMINIST CHEMIST. *Int. J. of Women's Studies (Canada) 1981 4(4): 420-430.*

Although faced with sex discrimination in her career in academe, this biochemist has achieved some measure of success and recognition, but more of it is due to her involvement in the women's movement, her leadership in the Association for Women in Science, and the altered climate of the 1970's with the feminist movement, than to her hard work and commitment to the sciences in the 50's and 60's.

BRONSON, FLORA ADELAIDE HOLCOMB

66. Leiber, Justin; Pickering, James; and White, Flora Bronson, ed. "MOTHER BY THE TENS": FLORA ADELAIDE HOLCOMB BRONSON'S ACCOUNT OF HER LIFE AS AN ILLINOIS SCHOOLTEACHER, POET, AND FARM WIFE, 1851-1927. *J. of the Illinois State Hist. Soc. 1983 76(4): 283-307.*

Memoirs of Flora Adelaide Holcomb Bronson, a native of Pennsylvania who lived and taught in Owosso, Michigan; Chicago; and central Illinois. After the death of her husband, Allen Walter Bronson, in 1918, she moved to Chicago and later to Lake Worth, Florida. Topics include farm life, poetry, rural religion, early sexuality, inadequate salaries for teachers, and death and illness.

BROWN, CHARLOTTE HAWKINS

67. Smith, Sandra N. and West, Earle H. CHARLOTTE HAWKINS BROWN. *J. of Negro Educ. 1982 51(3): 191-206.*

Charlotte Hawkins Brown (1883-1961) was founder and president of Palmer Memorial Institute in Greensboro, North Carolina, during 1902-52. Brown's varying groups of primary financial supporters caused her to shift the school's primary focus from vocational training to being an elite finishing school. By the 1940's, Brown shifted from accommodating to condemning discrimination. A self-conscious race leader working through women's clubs, Brown urged white women to support equal education and to respect black women and black class lines. She also encouraged black women to become cultured and to support black organizations.

BROWN, VIOLET GOLDSMITH

68. Brown, Violet. OVER THE RED DEER: LIFE OF A HOMESTEAD MISSIONARY. *Alberta History (Canada) 1985 33(3): 9-18.*

Prints the memoirs of Violet Goldsmith Brown, who arrived in Saskatchewan in 1905, married the Reverend John Brown, who became a Presbyterian minister the next year, and spent the rest of her life as a homesteading missionary. Follows the family's travels and settlement in Saskatchewan, and finally near the Red Deer River in Alberta. Illness and debt plagued the Browns, but farming and hunting in the area provided a fresh food supply.

BURNS, LUCY

69. Bland, Sidney R. "NEVER QUITE AS COMMITTED AS WE'D LIKE": THE SUFFRAGE MILITANCY OF LUCY BURNS. *J. of Long Island Hist. 1981 17(2): 4-23.*

Describes the suffrage career of Lucy Burns of Brooklyn, who served as "chief organizer, lobby head, newspaper editor, suffrage educator and teacher, orator, architect of the banner campaign, [and] rallying force and symbol" for the Congressional Union and its successor, the National Woman's Party, during 1913-19.

C

CALKINS, MARY WHITON

70. Furumuto, Laurel. MARY WHITON CALKINS (1863-1930): FOURTEENTH PRESIDENT OF THE AMERICAN PSYCHOLOGICAL ASSOCIATION. *J. of the Hist. of the Behavioural Sci. 1979 15(4): 346-356.*

Relatively little has been published about the life and contributions of Mary Whiton Calkins (1863-1930), 14th president of the American Psychological Association. A student of William James, Josiah Royce, and Hugo Munsterberg at

Harvard in the 1890's, Calkins completed all the requirements for the Ph.D. but was not granted the degree because she was a woman. Calkins's contributions to psychology include the invention of the paired-associate technique, the founding of one of the early psychological laboratories, and the development of a system of self-psychology. She published prolifically in both psychology and philosophy but was always more interested in theoretical and philosophical issues than in laboratory psychology. Although in the latter half of her career Calkins moved away from psychology into philosophy, her work contained a unifying theme: the emphasis on the importance of the self.

CAMERON, DONALDINA

71. McClain, Laurene Wu. DONALDINA CAMERON: A REAPPRAISAL. *Pacific Hist. 1983 27(3): 24-35.*

Reviews Donaldina Cameron's career with the Presbyterian Mission Home in San Francisco and her efforts to save illegally imported Chinese women from the slave trade. Her attitude toward the women exhibited little tolerance or sympathy and hampered her attempts to rehabilitate them. Although she spent 40 years in Chinatown she did not speak Chinese and referred to the Chinese as heathens.

CANNON, MARTHA HUGHES

72. Lieber, Constance L. "THE GOOSE HANGS HIGH": EXCERPTS FROM THE LETTERS OF MARTHA HUGHES CANNON. *Utah Hist. Q. 1980 48(1): 37-48.*

Martha Hughes Cannon (1857-1932) was the fourth polygamous wife of Angus Munn Cannon, president of the Salt Lake Stake of the Mormon Church. To prevent Angus Cannon's arrest for polygamy, Martha exiled herself to England during 1885-87. Her letters reveal loneliness, constant fear of exposure, fear of Cannon's arrest, and jealousy of other wives. The 1890 Manifesto allowed her to live openly in Salt Lake City and continue her medical career. In 1896 she became the first woman state senator in the United States.

CARLO, KATHLEEN

73. Bauman, Margaret. SCULPTOR KATHLEEN CARLO. *Alaska Journal 1982 12(1): 4-9.*

Reviews the career of Kathleen Carlo, an Alaskan sculptor and mask-maker whose work incorporates contemporary Western and traditional Athabascan influences. Carlo has held supervisory, instructional, and artist-in-residence posts in the Alaska interior and has gained prominence for her work in teak, birch, walnut, cedar, and other woods.

CARR, EMILY

74. Hirsch, Gilah Yelin. EMILY CARR. *Women's Studies 1978 6(1): 75-87.*

Emily Carr, the Canadian painter, acquired her fame posthumously. Her success, while she was alive, was handicapped by her Victorian upbringing, economic distress, and insular lifestyle. Carr attended the San Francisco Art School, Westminster School of Art in London, St. Ives school in Cornwall, and the Academie Colorossi in Paris. In Paris she came under the influence of impressionism and fauvism. Her early paintings documented Indian history, life, and art. Her later works pursued expression of spirituality. Many of Carr's paintings are in the National Gallery in Ottawa.

CARR, JEANNE CAROLINE SMITH

75. Apostol, Jane. JEANNE CARR: ONE WOMAN AND SUNSHINE. *Am. West 1978 15(4): 28-33, 62-63.*

Vermont-born Jeanne Caroline Smith Carr (1825-1903) was married to a medical scientist professor whose university assignments took them to California by way of Wisconsin. She became widely known as a feminist, author, botanist, officeholder, and educational reform activist. She met backwoods farmer John Muir while reporting on an exhibit of his inventions in Madison, Wisconsin. She became a close friend, correspondent, and mentor to Muir, whom she called "the Poet-Naturalist of our Coast."

CARVER, ADA JACK

76. Ford, Oliver. ADA JACK CARVER: THE BIOGRAPHY OF A SOUTHERN TRADITIONALIST. *Southern Studies 1979 18(2): 133-178.*

Ada Jack Carver's (1890-1972) short stories, novels, and plays in the 1920's, set in her native region of Natchitoches, Louisiana, were awarded literary prizes and enthusiastic public acclaim. Her reputation has not remained high because she was unable to transcend her own circumstances. Her works are suffused with southern romanticism, stock characters, and plots in which characters are unable to break out of their isolation or niche in society. She was unable to accept the realism in the literature of her time. Her stories concerned, for the most part, alienated or socially disenfranchised and aging women. Her most successful short story was "Redbone" in 1924.

CATHER, WILLA

77. Benson, Peter. WILLA CATHER AT THE *HOME MONTHLY*. *Biography 1981 4(3): 227-248.*

Willa Cather's first full-fledged literary apprenticeship came as managing editor of a women's domestic magazine where her writing germinated within the strictly defined genres of 19th-century popular journalism. However, critical neglect of these early writings and a serious error of fact, perpetuated by generations of scholars, have obscured these important influences on her early development.

78. Klug, Michael A. WILLA CATHER: BETWEEN RED CLOUD AND BYZANTIUM. *Can. Rev. of Am. Studies (Canada) 1981 12(3): 287-299.*

Writing early in the 20th century, American novelist Willa Cather (1876-1947) was troubled by the same spiritual and aesthetic contradictions that have frustrated 20th-century artists more recently. On the broadest level, Cather shares with her literary successors the conflicts inherent to the artistic desire for freedom and personal success and artists' opposite impulses to make social equality and human brotherhood paramount.

79. Lovering, Joseph P. THE FRIENDSHIP OF WILLA CATHER AND DOROTHY CANFIELD. *Vermont Hist. 1980 48(3): 145-154.*

From their collaboration in writing a prize short story in 1894 until Cather's death in 1947, the two authors corresponded with and visited each other, except for a decade of unexplained coolness between them from about 1905 to early 1916. The hiatus perhaps relates to the elder woman's direct rise from frontier Nebraska, with less social status or grace than Canfield, but earlier literary success.

80. Parks, B. K. A DEDICATION TO THE MEMORY OF WILLA CATHER, 1873-1947. *Arizona and the West 1979 21(3): 210-214.*

Throughout her years at the University of Nebraska, in journalism in Pennsylvania and publishing in New York, and in retirement, Willa Cather (1873-1947) wrote poetry, short stories, and novels. Her early writings reflected her bitterness toward the shallow crudeness of western (principally Nebraskan) and southwestern life. Later she came to view the West as a stage on which the fulfillment as well as the frustration of universal desires were played. She celebrated the "singular vitality" of European cultural contributions to the West.

CHABAN, TEKLIA

81. Woywitka, Anne B. A PIONEER WOMAN IN THE
LABOUR MOVEMENT.
Alberta Hist. (Canada) 1978 26(1): 10-16.

Teklia Chaban was born in the Ukraine. She moved to Alberta
in 1914, the year of her marriage. Her husband worked in the
Cardiff coal mines, 15 miles north of Edmonton. Follows the
family for the next 10 years, with agitation for a labor
organization, dealings with the United Mine Workers of
America, and strikes and violence in the early 1920's. She was
active in Ukrainian cultural movements that were part of the
labor efforts. In the mid-1920's the family moved to Edmonton,
and again was involved in agitation for labor recognition,
spending some time in jail and suffering periodic unemployment
for their efforts.

CHASE, JOSEPHINE STREEPER

82. Dix, Fae Decker, ed. THE JOSEPHINE DIARIES:
GLIMPSES OF THE LIFE OF JOSEPHINE STREEPER
CHASE, 1881-94.
Utah Hist. Q. 1978 46(2): 167-183.

Josephine Streeper Chase (1835-94) was the polygamous second
wife of George Ogden Chase in Centerville, Utah. She was the
mother of 15 children and one foster daughter, sunday school
teacher, successful manager of a large household, and faithful
church member. Her diary, covering 1881-94, is a priceless
journal of daily life in a busy Mormon home, describing with
surprising detail housecleaning, outdoor chores, baking,
preserving, churning, and hog killing. She voices the spirit and
ordeal of her time.

CHEESBOROUGH, ESTHER B.

83. Sutherland, Daniel E. THE RISE AND FALL OF
ESTHER B. CHEESBOROUGH: THE BATTLES OF A
LITERARY LADY.
South Carolina Historical Magazine 1983 84(1): 22-34.

Born in Charleston in 1826, Esther Cheesborough rose to prominence in Southern literary circles only to see her fame disappear and end her life in New York more than 20 years after the Civil War. Her literary style included intellectual honesty and a passion for naturalness. In her poems, short stories, and essays her characters survived lost or unfulfilled loves, which Cheesborough may have endured in her own life. During the Civil War her writing offered a view of Southern prisoners-of-war as well as deserters. Her social satire exposed "the absurdity of high society's values, taste, and conduct."

CHESNUT, MARY BOYKIN

84. Hoffert, Sylvia D. MARY BOYKIN CHESNUT: PRIVATE FEMINIST IN THE CIVIL WAR SOUTH. *Southern Studies 1977 16(1): 81-89.*

Mary Boykin Miller Chesnut (1823-1886) was from South Carolina and became a member of the Confederate social elite in Washington, Montgomery, Charleston, and Richmond. She kept a diary during 1860-65 in which she described Southern institutions in surprisingly blunt language. She never was a prominent public personality, nor did she express her ideas publicly. She is important as a private woman of the time who provides insights into how at least one woman felt about her life in the 19th century. Although she conformed outwardly to the accepted feminine roles of her day, she complained in her diary of male dominance, the humiliating position of married women, the personal limitations that motherhood imposed on women, and slavery. She disapproved of slavery and was totally against miscegenation.

85. Wiley, Bell I. DIARIST FROM DIXIE: MARY BOYKIN CHESNUT. *Civil War Times Illus. 1977 16(1): 22-32.*

Presents Mary Chesnut's memoirs, which are based on her recollections on a wartime journal. Her husband helped organize the Confederacy and elect president Jefferson Davis. The Chesnuts were close friends of the Davis's. Mary believed that the Confederacy's greatest weakness was the quarrelsomeness of its leaders due largely to the excessive individualism nurtured by the plantation. Little is known of her life after the war. She died in 1886.

CHILD, LYDIA MARIA

86. Holland, Patricia G. LYDIA MARIA CHILD AS A NINETEENTH-CENTURY PROFESSIONAL AUTHOR. *Studies in the Am. Renaissance 1981: 157-167.*

Traces the life and writing career of Lydia Maria Child, focusing on her involvement in the abolitionist and feminist movements. Throughout her life, Child directed her talents to the writing of books and articles that dealt with antislavery and women's issues, and with the special needs of children, as is evident in her role in the founding of *Juvenile Miscellany* in 1826, a periodical aimed at younger readers.

CHRISTIE, EMMA STRATTON

87. Peavy, Linda and Smith, Ursula. WOMEN IN WAITING IN THE WESTWARD MOVEMENT: PAMELIA DILLIN FERGUS AND EMMA STRATTON CHRISTIE. *Montana 1985 35(2): 2-17.*

The men who came to the Montana frontier frequently left their wives and families awaiting their return. With their husbands absent, these "women in waiting" assumed new responsibilities managing farms and businesses as well as households. The lives of these "widows" form a heretofore unexamined element of the frontier experience. The letters between Pamelia Dillin Fergus (1824-87) and James Fergus (1813-1902), and Emma Stratton Christie (1854-1921) and David Christie (1848-1920) portray the growth of self-reliance and independence among the "widows" as they endured their husbands' absences. These traits served them well when they rejoined their husbands on the frontier.

CHRISTIE, SARAH

88. Christie, Jean. "AN EARNEST ENTHUSIASM FOR EDUCATION": SARAH CHRISTIE STEVENS, SCHOOLWOMAN. *Minnesota Hist. 1983 48(6): 245-254.*

Sarah Christie, seen as a school girl, young teacher, mature wife, middle-aged political aspirant, and county superintendent of education offers yet another entree into the expectations, fears, and societal limitations common to late 19th-century women, at least those living in middling circumstances in the upper Midwest. Active in Baptist, Women's Christian Temperance Union, and Farmers' Alliance work in the late 1880's, she was able to gain election in Minnesota's Blue Earth County (Mankato) as one of the state's dozen female superintendent's in 1890. She lost the next two elections, as alliance strength split, and in the face of continued somewhat sexist arguments.

CLAPP, HANNAH KEZIAH

89. Totton, Kathryn Dunn. HANNAH KEZIAH CLAPP: THE LIFE AND CAREER OF A PIONEER NEVADA EDUCATOR, 1824-1908. *Nevada Hist. Soc. Q. 1977 20(3): 167-183.*

Describes the professional and political reform activities of Hannah Keziah Clapp in Nevada. From 1881 to 1901, she was a staff member of the University of Nevada, making significant contributions to the institution by upgrading and enlarging to University's library. She also worked for kindergartens in Reno and was active in women suffrage movements, among them the Nevada Equal Suffrage Association in which she was an officer.

CLAYTON, SUSAN HAINES

90. Hoar, Jay S. SUSAN HAINES CLAYTON, AMERICAN LADY, 1851-1948. *Oregon Hist. Q. 1983 84(2): 206-210.*

Examines milestones in the life of Susan Haines Clayton, who nursed the sick and wounded during the Civil War. While her family was living in Indiana, she, at the age of 10, was allowed by her mother to help nurse men at Camp Carrington at Indianapolis. Following her marriage to a former soldier in 1869, she homesteaded in southern Kansas and Montana and later was instrumental in organizing the Women's Relief Corps in those states.

COLBY, ABBY M.

91. Taylor, Sandra C. ABBY M. COLBY: THE CHRISTIAN RESPONSE TO SEXIST SOCIETY. *New England Q. 1979 52(1): 68-79.*

Women, who comprised two-thirds of the missionaries to Japan in the late 19th century, received lower pay than men and were only allowed to vote on matters of "women's work" within their organization. Abby M. Colby (1848-1917) was a feminist who served as a Congregational missionary in Japan between 1879 and 1914 and opposed these practices as much as she did Japanese practices of male-dominated marriages, concubinage, and prostitution.

COLLINS, MARY CLEMENTINE

92. Borst, John C. THE MARY C. COLLINS FAMILY PAPERS AT THE SOUTH DAKOTA HISTORICAL RESOURCE CENTER. *South Dakota History 1982 12(4): 248-253.*

Traces the life and career of Mary Clementine Collins, a missionary to the Sioux in South Dakota during 1875-1910, and describes the contents of the Mary C. Collins Family Papers which are divided into two categories: those dealing with Mary C. Collins; and those concerning the family of Ethel Collins Jacobsen, her niece (who was also involved in mission work among the Sioux). Included in the Mary C. Collins material are correspondence dealing with various aspects of mission life and the problems involved in gaining fair treatment and legal rights for the Indians, a short autobiography, diaries, genealogical information, and photographs. The Ethel Jacobsen material contains diaries of Ethel and her husband Elias, correspondence, genealogical information, and miscellaneous folders. The material is valuable for the study of 19th- and early 20th-century missionary efforts among the Sioux Indians of South Dakota.

93. Clow, Richmond L., ed. AUTOBIOGRAPHY OF MARY C. COLLINS, MISSIONARY TO THE WESTERN SIOUX. *South Dakota Historical Collections 1982 41: 1-66.*

Consists of the autobiography of Mary Clementine Collins, who describes her work as a missionary of the Congregational Church to the Western Sioux in South Dakota from 1875 to 1910. Collins discusses her religious upbringing, her assignment to the Oahe Mission, the condition of the Indians' lives near the mission, and her memories of friends and acquaintances, both white and Indian. Among the prominent figures she encountered were Sitting Bull and the many Indian agents assigned to the Sioux agencies in North and South Dakota. By 1900 Collins began to question government policies intended to lead to Indian self-sufficiency, and she aired her complaints in letters to the Indian commissioners and at the Lake Mohonk Conferences.

COOKE, GRACE MACGOWAN

94. Gaston, Kay Baker. THE MACGOWAN GIRLS. *California Hist. 1980 59(2): 116-125.*

Traces the careers of Grace MacGowan Cooke (1863-1944) and her sister Alice MacGowan (1858-1947), prolific authors of popular novels, short stories, and poems. Born in Ohio and raised in Tennessee, the sisters joined Upton Sinclair for a time at his literary colony in New Jersey before coming to Carmel-by-the-Sea, California, in December 1908. For more than three decades the sisters collaborated with each other, with other writers, and in single authorship to produce a body of literature which, while not profound, brought them financial success. As literary figures they were on intimate terms with Sinclair Lewis (who worked as their secretary for a time), Jack London, George Sterling, and other west coast luminaries.

COOLBRITH, INA

95. Herr, Pamela. PORTRAIT FOR A WESTERN ALBUM. *Am. West 1978 15(3): 30-31.*

The family of Josephine Donna Smith (1841-1928) fled from the violence and persecution the Mormons suffered in Nauvoo, Illinois. In her teen years in Los Angeles, California, she became a recognized poet and also experienced a disastrous marriage. She changed her name to Ina Coolbrith and hid the secrets of her Mormon background and unfortunate marriage. She relocated in San Francisco, and her fame spread. Her energies were soon consumed, however, when she accepted full-time employment to support four relatives and friends. Despite decreased literary production, she was honored by California as its poet laureate.

COPPIN, FANNY JACKSON

96. Perkins, Linda M. HEED LIFE'S DEMANDS: THE EDUCATIONAL PHILOSOPHY OF FANNY JACKSON COPPIN. *J. of Negro Educ. 1982 51(3): 181-190.*

Fanny Jackson Coppin was the principal of the Female Department during 1865-69 and then principal during 1869-1902 of the Institute for Colored Youth in Philadelphia, Pennsylvania. She abolished tuition to reach poor students and developed a normal school with a student teaching program without sacrificing liberal arts to vocational education. She also urged the wider black community to avoid elitism and to practice racial solidarity and service through self-help by establishing such homes as she helped start for elderly and young black women.

CORY, FANNY Y.

97. Cooney, Bob and Dodgson, Sayre Cooney. FANNY CORY COONEY: MONTANA MOTHER AND ARTIST. *Montana 1980 30(3): 2-17.*

Fanny Young Cory Cooney (1877-1972) was an illustrator, artist, and cartoonist, 1896-1956. Under the name Fanny Y. Cory, her works appeared in such periodicals as *Life*, *Century*, *Harper's Bazaar*, and *Saturday Evening Post*, plus dozens of children's books. She interrupted her artistic career when she married Fred Cooney in 1904. They raised four children on a ranch near Canyon Ferry, Montana, and she was a devoted mother. To help finance education for her children, she returned to art and began two nationally syndicated cartoon strips, *Sonnysayings* and *Little Miss Muffet*, which ran in newspapers from 1926 to 1956.

COTTEN, SALLIE SOUTHALL

98. Stephenson, William. HOW SALLIE SOUTHALL COTTEN BROUGHT NORTH CAROLINA TO THE CHICAGO WORLD'S FAIR OF 1893.
North Carolina Hist. Rev. 1981 58(4): 364-383.

Sallie Southall Cotten (1846-1929), wife of a planter and rural store owner in Pitt County, North Carolina, rose to statewide prominence between 1890 and 1893 as alternate lady manager for North Carolina to the World's Columbian Exposition (Chicago, 1893). A moderate feminist with no experience in public affairs, Cotten successfully took charge of several important matters including fund raising for a North Carolina building at the fair and locating and designing exhibit materials. She also served as unofficial North Carolina hostess during the fair. Her work on the fair launched Cotten's national career in public service, especially in the National Congress of Mothers and the General Federation of Women's Clubs.

COUNTRYMAN, GRATIA ALTA

99. Rohde, Nancy Freeman. GRATIA ALTA COUNTRYMAN: LIBRARIAN AND REFORMER.
Stuhler, Barbara and Kreuter, Gretchen, ed.
Women of Minnesota: Selected Biographical Essays (St. Paul: Minnesota Historical Society Press, 1977): 173-189.

Gratia Alta Countryman (1866-1953) attended the University of Minnesota where she was an active student leader and member of Phi Beta Kappa. After graduating, she became one of six assistants hired to open and operate the new Minneapolis Public Library. Gratia soon became head of the catalog department. During 1904-36 she was the head librarian, the first woman to direct a major library in the United States. Countryman especially encouraged extended library services to meet the needs of all sectors of society. She also agitated for state library laws, promoted the Minnesota Library Association, served on the State Library Commission, and was nationally renowned for her work. She served on the council, executive board, and as president of the American Library Association. A popular speaker, Countryman lectured not only on library subjects but also on woman's suffrage, social reform, and international peace. She helped organize the Minneapolis Women's Welfare League and the Business Women's Club. In 1936, she chaired the national convention of the Women's International League for Peace and Freedom. A dedicated, efficient, and decisive librarian, social reformer, and civic leader, Countryman remained active after her retirement. She died on 26 July 1953.

COWAN, MARGERY JACOBY

100. Coleman, Alice Cowan. MISS JACOBY: 19TH CENTURY EDUCATOR, 20TH CENTURY GUARDIAN OF EXCELLENCE.
Montana 1978 28(2): 36-49.

Margery Jacoby Cowan came to Montana in 1883. She grew up in the Highwood Mountains near Fort Benton, and eventually became a school teacher in the vicinity. In 1894 she was elected Superintendent of Schools for Chouteau County. She worked vigorously to improve schools and teacher training during her four years in office. In 1899 Margery Jacoby married William T. Cowan, a Box Elder merchant and political leader. She abandoned her career, devoting full time to her responsibilities as wife and mother of four children. She supported her husband's career as postmaster, US Land Commissioner, joint founder of Northern Montana College, and "father of the Marias River Irrigation Project." Largely through Cowan's persistent efforts, Congress passed legislation financing construction of the Tiber Dam in 1952. William Cowan died the year before, but Margery Cowan attended ground-breaking ceremonies for Tiber

Dam to indicate her long-standing support for her husband's work and for the prosperity of north-central Montana.

CRANDALL, PRUDENCE

101. Davis, Rodney O. PRUDENCE CRANDALL, SPIRITUALISM, AND POPULIST-ERA REFORM IN KANSAS. *Kansas Hist. 1980 3(4): 239-254.*

Prudence Crandall (1803-90) came to Elk County, Kansas, in 1877. For 13 years she was a leader in the movements for women's rights and prohibition. Her efforts in behalf of these old-fashioned issues more than offset popular resentment of her belief in spiritualist ideas that ran counter to the tenets of Christianity. She made no public appeal for support but advanced her interests in spiritualism by holding small meetings in her home. Her leading disciples waged a major effort in support of spiritualism from 1890 to 1895. Long opposed by organized clergymen, spiritualists now faced a stronger opponent. In the 1840's it was possible to have great topics discussed at any American crossroads, but by 1890 such theorizing appeared ludicrous. Knowledge was becoming the preserve of trained academics.

CRAWFORD, ISABEL

102. Mondello, Salvatore. ISABEL CRAWFORD: THE MAKING OF A MISSIONARY. *Foundations 1978 21(4): 322-339.*

Presents the early life and education of Isabel Crawford, a missionary of the Women's American Baptist Home Missionary Society. Born in Canada in 1865, she became interested in the plight of the Indians through various family moves while a child. She received her training in Chicago, during which time she did considerable work in the slums. In June, 1893, she received word that she had been appointed to work as a missionary among the Kiowas of Elk Creek, Indian Territory.

CROUTER, NATALIE

103. Crouter, Natalie. FORBIDDEN DIARY.
Am. Heritage 1979 30(3): 78-95.

Natalie Crouter, husband Jerry, and their two children, ages 12
and 10, were captured in the Philippines by the Japanese shortly
after Pearl Harbor. Natalie's diary, which had to be kept hidden
from her captors, survived to recount some of the family's
experiences during more than three years of internment.

CUNNINGHAM, AGNES "SIS"

104. Schrems, Suzanne H. RADICALISM AND SONG.
Chronicles of Oklahoma 1984 62(2): 190-206.

Agnes "Sis" Cunningham was born to an Oklahoma farm family
that lost its heavily mortgaged land to bank foreclosure during
the late 1930's. Her father and brother joined a grass-roots
socialist movement which drew some of its doctrine from
Commonwealth Labor College, a radical labor school in Mena,
Arkansas. While attending the school, Agnes wrote plays known
as "agitprop," which promoted political agitation and
propaganda. With her Red Dust Players, she presented political
plays complete with unionist songs of her own composition.
Agnes continued her involvement with folk music into the
1950's and 1960's, when she promoted young performers such
as Bob Dylan and Phil Ochs.

D

DAVIDSON, LUCRETIA AND MARGARET

105. Medoff, Jeslyn. DIVINE CHILDREN: THE
DAVIDSON SISTERS AND THEIR MOTHER.
J. of the Rutgers U. Lib. 1984 46(1): 16-27.

Discusses the letters and notebooks of Lucretia and Margaret
Davidson, American sister-poets of the early 19th century who
died of consumption in adolescence. The Davidsons'
sentimental and uplifting verse, combined with their invalidism

and death, made them heroines of a posthumous literary cult led by their powerful mother, Margaret Miller Davidson. In a period of renewed interest in the cultural tradition of the American woman poet, these child-poets suggest how the female poetic gift became associated with death and the elegiac mode.

DAVIS, ALICE BROWN

106. Waldowski, Paula. ALICE BROWN DAVIS: A LEADER OF HER PEOPLE. *Chronicles of Oklahoma 1980-81 58(4): 455-463.*

Alice Brown Davis (1852-1935) was born into an illustrious mixed-blood Seminole family which represented the pro-acculturation faction of the tribe. Educated by missionaries, she devoted her life to Indian education and served as superintendent of the Seminole girls' school called Emahaka Mission. Despite her emphasis upon teaching white ways to Indian children, she struggled to maintain total Indian control over the school but ultimately lost the battle. In 1922 she became the first woman to serve as principal chief of the Seminole Nation.

DAVIS, VARINA HOWELL

107. Dolensky, Suzanne T. VARINA HOWELL DAVIS, 1889 TO 1906: THE YEARS ALONE. *Journal of Mississippi History 1985 47(2): 90-109.*

Biographers have largely ignored the years of Varina Howell Davis after the death of her husband, Jefferson Davis. She was active after 1889 both as a literary figure and a planter, and tried to shape the image of her husband through her writings and by burying him in Richmond, Virginia. In her attempts to manage Jefferson Davis's image, as well as her departure from the South to New York City to develop her literary career, she became involved in controversy with Mississippians and those faithful to the Southern cause.

DENSMORE, FRANCES

108. Archabal, Nina Marchetti. FRANCES DENSMORE: PIONEER IN THE STUDY OF AMERICAN INDIAN MUSIC. Stuhler, Barbara and Kreuter, Gretchen, ed. *Women of Minnesota: Selected Biographical Essays (St. Paul: Minnesota Historical Society Press, 1977): 94-115.*

Frances Densmore (1867-1957) was born and raised in Red Wing, Minnesota, where the sight of Indians was common. Densmore was formally trained in 18th- and 19th-century European music; her scholarly research in Native American music made her a pioneer in ethnomusicology. Alice Cunningham Fletcher and John Comfort Fillmore especially influenced Densmore when she began her studies of Indian music in the 1890's. From then until her death in 1957, Densmore studied, recorded, analyzed, and published monographs on the music of the Chippewa, Teton Sioux, Papago, Arapaho, Ute, Mandan, Zuni, and many other Indians. The Bureau of American Ethnology financially supported her work, and she collected more than 2,400 wax cylinders of Native American music. Densmore gradually evolved a theory and understanding of Indian music which appreciated its cultural context and recognized it as "profoundly different" from Western musical tradition.

DESHA, MARY

109. Klotter, James C. and Klotter, Freda Campbell. MARY DESHA, ALASKAN SCHOOLTEACHER OF 1888. *Pacific Northwest Q. 1980 71(2): 78-86.*

Presents excerpts from the letters of Mary Desha (1850-1911), who in 1888, set out from her comfortable parents' home in Lexington, Kentucky, for the frontier settlement of Sitka, Alaska, where she had accepted a teaching position. Many of her letters praised the natural beauty of Alaska, but she simultaneously held a strong contempt for most of the Indian, Russian, and Yankee population encountered there. In some ways Mary Desha proved flexible in adapting to frontier conditions, but she could not escape the biases endemic to a true, unreconstructed southerner. Following her return from Alaska, she became heavily involved with the Daughters of the

American Revolution and the United Daughters of the Confederacy.

DICKINSON, EMILY

110. Burbick, Joan. "ONE UNBROKEN COMPANY": RELIGION AND EMILY DICKINSON. *New England Q. 1980 53(1): 62-75.*

Examines religious life at Mount Holyoke College during the time Emily Dickinson (1830-86) studied there. Concludes that, contrary to some biographers' views, she did not rebel against religion. Her religion was "fused with the issue of friendship" and for a time she feared that her friends' conversion would separate them from her. For Dickinson "the bonds of friendship determine meaning here as well as in the Christian heaven . .. " and her reaction against religion was "not based on astance of heroic individualism, but on a continued struggle to avoid isolation and to cement the bonds of friendship."

111. Klein, Maury. THE ENIGMA OF EMILY. *Am. Hist. Illus. 1977 12(8): 4-11.*

Emily Dickinson (1830-86) was born and died in Amherst, Massachusetts. She rejected church membership in 1848 and lived a secluded life. She never left Amherst after 1865, and rarely left her house. Her inability to meet anyone who could deal with her intellectual and emotional energy, her intensity, and her acute perception and sensitivity account for her seclusion. She found a release in writing letters to her friends (more than 1000 survive) and in her poetry (1,775 poems and fragments have been collected).

112. Morris, Adelaide K. TWO SISTERS HAVE I: EMILY DICKINSON'S VINNIE AND SUSAN. *Massachusetts Rev. 1981 22(2): 323-332.*

Describes the two most important women in Emily Dickinson's life: her natural sister, Lavinia Norcross Dickinson (b. ca. 1832), familiarly referred to as Vinnie, and her brother's wife, Susan Gilbert Dickinson, commonly called Sue, her lifelong friend and fascination. The three women were neighbors for 30 years, sharing each other's sufferings and triumphs. Sue represented the heavenly in Emily's life, Vinnie the earthly. These two complementary yet contradictory influences helped keep Emily on an even keel. Emily referred to Vinnie's world as a prose world and to Sue's as a poetry world. Relations between Vinnie and Sue exploded after Emily died, since Emily's role as arbitrator was vacant. Covers ca. 1850-86.

DICKSON, ANNA MAE

113. Watriss, Wendy. "IT'S SOMETHING INSIDE YOU." *Southern Exposure 1977 4(4): 76-81.*

Anna Mae Dickson emerged as a black community leader in east Texas during the 1950's and became especially active in school affairs. Compelled at an early age to labor as a cotton fieldhand, Dickson later engaged in domestic service. This experience provided her with considerable insight into the white community. Her present role as community activist rests on her belief that it is important to maintain links between the black and white communities and to have black representation in community organizations.

DIX, DOROTHEA

114. Cullen, Joseph. DOROTHEA DIX: FORGOTTEN CRUSADER. *Am. Hist. Illus. 1978 13(4): 11-17.*

Dorothea Dix (1802-87) effected sweeping reforms in the care of the insane in America, Europe, and even Japan. In 1841, when she became interested in the problem, it was widely believed that the insane were insensitive to cold and other discomfort, and they were treated accordingly. Dix always acted alone and sought no publicity. She would investigate conditions in a particular state, then present an eloquently written memorial to the legislature through a sympathetic member. Successful with state legislatures, she failed repeatedly to get federal assistance for the insane. Her service during the Civil War as Superintendent of Women Nurses for the Union Army was not a success, partly for reasons of temperament. She was active in behalf of the insane until her death in 1887.

DODGE, MARY ABIGAIL

115. Beasley, Maurine. MARY ABIGAIL DODGE: "GAIL HAMILTON" AND THE PROCESS OF SOCIAL CHANGE. *Essex Inst. Hist. Collections 1980 116(2): 82-100.*

The writings of Mary Abigail Dodge (1833-96), a pioneer female journalist of the 19th century, fell into obscurity after her death. Using the pseudonym "Gail Hamilton," she provided in her essays a witty, feminine interpretation of self-reliance and individual improvement based on the philosophy of Ralph Waldo Emerson, whom she knew personally. Examines her life, her writings, and her living arrangements with the James G. Bailey family in Washington, D.C.

DONNELLY, KATHARINE MCCAFFREY

116. Kreuter, Gretchen. KATE DONNELLY VERSUS THE CULT OF TRUE WOMANHOOD.
Stuhler, Barbara and Kreuter, Gretchen, ed.
Women of Minnesota: Selected Biographical Essays (St. Paul: Minnesota Historical Society Pr., 1977): 20-33.

Traces the life of Katharine McCaffrey Donnelly (1833-94) and discusses her marriage to Ignatius Donnelly. Full of energy, humor, forthrightness, advice, and warmth, Kate's letters to her husband reveal her political acumen, concern for their family, events in their daily lives, and their financial circumstances. Born in Philadelphia, Kate spent most of her life there and in Minnesota where she managed the farm while her husband pursued politics.

DOOLITTLE, CLARA MATTESON

117. Hickey, James T., ed. AN ILLINOIS FIRST FAMILY: THE REMINISCENCES OF CLARA MATTESON DOOLITTLE.
J. of the Illinois State Hist. Soc. 1976 69(1): 2-16.

Provides reminiscences of Mrs. James Doolittle, daughter of Illinois governor Joel Matteson (1852-56). She describes the family's comfortable and patrician style of life in Illinois and abroad in the 1850's and throughout the Civil War. The editor presents a history of the first governor's mansion, 1843-56, money for which was not appropriated until more than 20 years after statehood. The editor also describes the life-size marble statue of Stephen A. Douglas by Leonard Volk; it was first used as a touring campaign prop.

DUNBAR-NELSON, ALICE

118. Hull, Gloria T. ALICE DUNBAR-NELSON: DELAWARE WRITER AND WOMAN OF AFFAIRS. *Delaware Hist. 1976 17(2): 87-103.*

 Presents a biography of Alice Dunbar-Nelson, who was active in black educational and philanthropic enterprises and community affairs in Wilmington. Her poetry and prose writing, dominated by themes of love and war, bridged the distance separating her husband, Paul Laurence Dunbar, and the dialect writers of the Harlem Renaissance. Dunbar-Nelson used regionalism and local color, and, unlike other black writers, she attempted the short story as her main prose medium, helping create a black short story tradition.

DUPONT, VICTORINE

119. Johnson, Mary. VICTORINE DU PONT: HEIRESS TO THE EDUCATIONAL DREAM OF PIERRE SAMUEL DU PONT DE NEMOURS. *Delaware Hist. 1980 19(2): 88-105.*

Argues that Victorine du Pont (b. 1792), the granddaughter of Pierre Samuel du Pont de Nemours, the physiocrat, imbibed du Pont de Nemours' thinking on the need for democratic education and translated her experience of growing up in France to the upbringing of the du Pont family in America and to the mill towns of the Brandywine region. She became an advocate of primary education in the rural manufacturing districts of the middle Atlantic region, working particularly with the American Sunday School Movement. Her chief legacy was the Brandywine Manufacturers' Sunday School, incorporated in 1817, which embodied the du Pont concept that learning should be pleasurable not corporal. Her other legacy was the liberal education of the du Pont family, which guided them even as they attended formal schools.

E

EDDY, MARY BAKER

120. Klein, Janice. ANN LEE AND MARY BAKER EDDY: THE PARENTING OF NEW RELIGIONS. *J. of Psychohistory 1979 6(3): 361-375.*

The Christian Science and Shaker religions, founded by Mary Baker Eddy and Ann Lee, respectively, had roots in the personal lives of their founders as well as in their social milieux. Focuses on the former, comparing the life experiences of Eddy and Lee, and suggests ways in which those experiences affected the theologies of the two religions.

121.

Silberger, Julius, Jr. MARY BAKER EDDY. *Am. Heritage 1980 32(1): 56-64.*

Adapted from the author's recently published biography of Mary Baker Eddy (1821-1910), the founder and developer of Christian Science, who began her writing and founded the church in 1875 after a long and often unhappy earlier life. From the beginning, she sought to rid the church of any competitors to her own position. She founded the *Christian Science Monitor* in 1908, two years before her death.

EDE, SUSANNA

122. Zimmerman, Barbara Baker and Carstensen, Vernon. PIONEER WOMAN IN SOUTHWESTERN WASHINGTON TERRITORY: THE RECOLLECTIONS OF SUSANNA MARIA SLOVER MC FARLAND PRICE EDE. *Pacific Northwest Q. 1976 67(4): 137-150.*

Reminiscences of Susanna Ede (1854-1937), whose pioneer life was spent along the lower Chehalis River, Grays Harbor, and the Copalis Beach area of Washington Territory. Widowed by William McFarland at age 26, she twice remarried, first to Dr. J. B. Price, physician at the Quinault Indian Agency, and later to Walter Ede whom she later divorced. Susanna described her log cabin life during the 1870's, her position as teacher and government interpreter at the Quinault Agency, bouts with timber wolves, and the production of home remedies and canned foods.

EDMONDS, SARAH EMMA

123. Lammers, Pat and Boyce, Amy. ALIAS FRANKLIN THOMPSON: A FEMALE IN THE RANKS. *Civil War Times Illus. 1984 22(9): 24-31.*

Sarah Emma Edmonds employed pseudonyms and disguises in order to serve in the 2d Michigan Volunteer Infantry during the Civil War; her talent for hiding her true identity again proved useful when she became a Union spy, infiltrating Confederate defenses by means of a variety of disguises.

EDWARDS, INDIA WALKER

124. Morgan, Georgia Cook. INDIA EDWARDS: DISTAFF POLITICIAN OF THE TRUMAN ERA. *Missouri Hist. Rev. 1984 78(3): 293-310.*

Prints a biography of India Walker Edwards, who worked with the Women's Division and the Democratic National Committee, bringing feminism into US political leadership years before it became fashionable. She used her journalistic experience from the Chicago *Tribune* to write speeches and news releases for the Democratic Party. She also brought other women into important positions, until Stephen Mitchell froze them out in 1953.

EGG, ELEANOR

125. Jable, J. Thomas. ELEANOR EGG: PATERSON'S TRACK-AND-FIELD HEROINE. *New Jersey History 1984 102(3-4): 68-84.*

Eleanor Egg, the daughter of vaudevillians, demonstrated her prowess at athletics during her grammar school years. Later, Egg and her contemporaries competed through the Paterson Girls' Recreation Association (PGRA) in track meets from New York to California. Even though she did well in many events during the 1920's and early 1930's, injuries kept her from US Olympic teams in 1928 and 1932. Because of her athletic talents and agreeable personality, Paterson officials used her as a focus of city boosterism.

EHRMAN, THERESA

126. Strauss, Leon L., ed. BELOVED SCRIBE: LETTERS OF THERESA EHRMAN. *Western States Jewish Hist. Q. 1979 12(1): 39-62; 1980 12(2): 142-160, 12(3): 229-245.*

Part I. Theresa Ehrman (1884-1967) was related to Leo and Gertrude Stein, Americans who lived in Paris, France, in the center of a literary and artistic community. Theresa went to Paris to advance her training as a pianist. She lived with Michael and Sarah Stein, Leo's brother and sister-in-law. Among her acquaintances were Pablo Casals and other noted musicians of the era. Part II. In the summer of 1904, Theresa Ehrman toured Switzerland, Italy, Holland, Belgium, and Germany with her relatives Mike and Sarah Stein. In Germany, she visited her father's brother and sister. Back in Paris in October, she continued piano studies with Harold Bauer. Part III. Late in 1904, Theresa broke off her romantic relationship with Pablo Casals, but they maintained a lifelong friendship. Her piano studies continued in Paris with Therese Chaigneau and Harold Bauer. After her return home to San Francisco in 1905, Theresa began her career as an accompanist and piano teacher. She was a close friend to many outstanding musicians, composers, and conductors. In her last years she lived in the San Francisco Bay area.

EIFERT, VIRGINIA S.

127. Hallwas, John E. THE ACHIEVEMENT OF VIRGINIA S. EIFERT. *J. of the Illinois State Hist. Soc. 1978 71(2): 82-106.*

Virginia S. Eifert (1911-66) of Springfield, Illinois, was one of the most widely known midwestern artists and nature writers of the 20th century. Her canon includes 19 books and hundreds of short articles; among her finest are the essays she wrote as editor of the Illinois State Museum magazine, *Living Museum.*

EQUI, MARIE

128. Krieger, Nancy. QUEEN OF THE BOLSHEVIKS: THE HIDDEN HISTORY OF DR. MARIE EQUI. *Radical America 1983 17(5): 55-73.*

Dr. Marie Equi was a powerful individual who manifested determination in her personal, professional, and political life. As a physician, she built a working-class practice. As a political activist, she emerged as a radical when Oregon's Industrial Commission betrayed its own guidelines in the settlement of a 1913 strike involving women workers at the Oregon Packing Company in Portland. Her antiwar stance brought trial and conviction under the Sedition Act just after the Armistice. After emerging from prison, she continued her medical practice and her radicalism through the 1920's until a crippling heart attack in 1930.

ESSIG, MAUDE FRANCES

129. Woolley, Alma S. A HOOSIER NURSE IN FRANCE: THE WORLD WAR I DIARY OF MAUDE FRANCES ESSIG. *Indiana Magazine of History 1986 82(1): 37-68.*

Maude Frances Essig served as an American Red Cross nurse for almost two years during World War I. She worked at a number of field hospitals in France and described the variety of medical and social tasks assigned to the nurses. Discusses the relationships of military nurses and doctors, and describes the medical treatment of the various injuries suffered by soldiers. The hours of work were long and the working conditions far worse than in any American hospital Essig had worked at. Following the Armistice of 11 November 1918, the nurses dealt frequently with injured German prisioners of war. After returning to the United States, Essig had a long professional career in public and military hospitals.

F

FARNHAM, ELIZA

130. Hallwas, John E. ELIZA FARNHAM'S LIFE IN PRAIRIE LAND. *Old Northwest 1981-82 7(4): 295-324.*

Discusses Eliza Farnham's frontier memoir, *Life in Prairie Land* (1846), which was based on her experiences in the Illinois River Valley during 1835-40. The little known work deserves more critical interest than it has received. Her description of the landscape and culture of Illinois accurately displays life in the region. The vividly written account is part autobiography, part travel literature, and part extended essay.

FELTON, REBECCA LATIMER

131. Rogers, Evelyna Keadle. FAMOUS GEORGIA WOMEN: REBECCA LATIMER FELTON. *Georgia Life 1978 5(1): 34-35.*

Rebecca Latimer Felton (1835-1930), a resident of Georgia, was appointed as the first woman senator in the US Senate in 1922; discusses her career in politics and her participation in the fight for woman suffrage, 1860's-1922.

FIELDE, ADELE M.

132. Hoyt, Frederick B. "WHEN A FIELD WAS FOUND TOO DIFFICULT FOR A MAN, A WOMAN SHOULD BE SENT": ADELE M. FIELDE IN ASIA, 1865-1890. *Historian 1982 44(3): 314-334.*

Adele M. Fielde, a transitional figure, illustrates the changing emphasis of the Protestant mission movement from wives to single women as evangelists. Recounts Fielde's life, including her introduction to the Orient in 1865, her missionary work as an American Baptist in Siam, her assignment to Swatow in China in 1872, and her permanent return to the United States in 1890. The major focus of her life as both a missionary and reformer was the condition of women and the reformation of society.

FOOTE, MARY HALLOCK

133. Paul, Rodman W. WHEN CULTURE CAME TO BOISE: MARY HALLOCK FOOTE IN IDAHO. *Idaho Yesterdays 1976 20(2): 2-12.*

Mary Hallock Foote, born in New York state, married an engineer and followed him West after having established herself as a successful magazine artist. Her stories and sketches depicted her western experiences even though she always regarded herself as an exile from civilization and culture. Includes paintings by Foote first published in *Century Illustrated Monthly Magazine* 1888-90.

FORT, CORNELIA CLARK

134. Tanner, Doris Brinker. CORNELIA FORT: A WASP IN WORLD WAR II, PART I. *Tennessee Hist. Q. 1981 40(4): 381-394.*

Cornelia Clark Fort (1919-43), born into the social elite of Nashville, Tennessee, became a pioneering woman flyer when she returned home after graduating from Sarah Lawrence College in 1939. She was in the air as a flight instructor over

Pearl Harbor when the Japanese attacked. She returned home a celebrity. In 1942 she entered the army's Ferrying Division of the Air Transport Command.

FOX, RUTH MAY

135. Thatcher, Linda, ed. "I CARE NOTHING FOR POLITICS": RUTH MAY FOX, FORGOTTEN SUFFRAGIST. *Utah Hist. Q. 1981 49(3): 239-253.*

Ruth May Fox spent most of her adult life as both mother and speaker for the suffrage movement in Utah. Her interest in the suffrage movement began when she joined the Utah Women's Press Club and Reaper's Club as a writer and acquaintance of other women (Dr. Ellis R. Shipp, Dr. Ellen B. Ferguson, Emma McVicker, and Emmeline B. Wells) who proved to be major influences on her desire to improve the role of women in society. During the latter portion of the 19th century, she became active in the Utah Woman Suffrage Association, Salt Lake County Republican Committee, Second Precinct Ladies Republican Club, Deseret Agricultural & Manufacturing Society, Traveler's Aid Society, and Young Ladies' Mutual Improvement Association. Most of her later activities were with the Young Ladies' Mutual Improvement Association. A portion of her diary reveals her constant traveling and speaking to improve women's rights within the political confines of the community. She died in 1958 with little recognition for her past efforts.

FRANK, SARAH VASEN

136. Clar, Reva. FIRST JEWISH WOMAN PHYSICIAN OF LOS ANGELES. *Western States Jewish Hist. Q. 1981 14(1): 66-75.*

Dr. Sarah Vasen (1870-1944), served as the first superintendent and resident physician of the Kaspare Cohn Hospital, forefunner of Cedars-Sinai Medical Center in Los Angeles. Vasen's superintendency began in 1905 and ended in 1910 when she began a private practice specializing in maternity cases. Her marriage to Saul Frank in 1912 ended her professional career.

FRAZER, MARY

137. Parry, Edward Owen. MARY FRAZER: HEROINE OF THE AMERICAN REVOLUTION. *Daughters of the Am. Revolution Mag. 1979 113(7): 766-775.*

Briefly outlines the American Revolution, detailing the life of Mary Frazer (1745-1830), who was active defending her home at Thornsbury, Pennsylvania; she crossed British lines to help American prisoners of war in Philadelphia and brought supplies to the Army during the winter at Valley Forge. Traces the military involvement of her husband, Persifor Frazer, in the war.

FREMONT, JESSIE BENTON

138. Herr, Pamela. THE LIFE OF JESSIE BENTON FREMONT. *Am. West 1979 16(2): 4-13, 59-63.*

Jessie Anne Benton (1824-1902) was educated and influenced by the political, cultural, and westward-dreaming family life of Senator Thomas Hart Benton in Washington and in their Missouri home. Her marriage to John Charles Fremont made her the "passionate connecting link" between the ambitious young army explorer and his powerful senator father-in-law. Having served as her father's secretary and assistant, Jessie served her husband in the same capacity through his stormy military and political career. She "shared in her husband's life more fully than most women, learning to accept the limitations that both her sex and fate enforced."

FREY, LORAINE JOHNSON

139. Frey, Loraine Johnson. GROWING UP DURING HARD TIMES. *Rendezvous 1984 20(1): 48-54.*

The author describes growing up poor in rural Idaho during the Great Depression. Her family was forced to move and had to rent a farm near Pocatello after their family farm was lost by foreclosure in 1931. Despite severe financial problems, she and her family, through hard work, cooperation, and courage, managed to survive as well as help her earn a teaching certificate at the University of Idaho, Southern Branch.

FULLER, LILLIAN BECK

140. Hawkins, Joellen Beck W., ed. PUBLIC HEALTH NURSING IN CHICAGO IN THE 1920S: THE REMINISCENCES OF LILLIAN BECK FULLER, R.N. *J. of the Illinois State Hist. Soc. 1983 76(3): 195-204.*

Lillian Beck Fuller studied and practiced nursing in Chicago. Presents reminiscences of her studies at Presbyterian Hospital and her service with the Visiting Nurse Association in the Hull-House, Little Italy, Sleepy Valley, and Jewish districts, and at the Home for Destitute Crippled Children. She was the first nurse with the Visiting Nurse Association permitted to retain her position after marriage. She left Chicago when her husband, a doctor, began advanced studies in Philadelphia. Upon his later hospitalization, Fuller returned to Minnesota, where she served as a school and camp nurse.

FULLER, MARGARET

141. Hlus, Carolyn. MARGARET FULLER, TRANSCEN-DENTALIST: A RE-ASSESSMENT. *Canadian Review of Am. Studies (Canada) 1985 16(1): 1-13.*

Historical consensus accords American journalist and feminist Margaret Fuller (1810-50) a second-rate place in the transcendentalist movement. Nonetheless, her contemporaries judged her a major figure in Boston and New York intellectual circles from 1836 to 1844, and she actually became a prominent transcendentalist. Her most important contribution to the movement was her use of transcendentalist theories to explain the natural rights of women. Her most influential writing was *Women in the Nineteenth Century* (1845).

142. vonFrank, Albert J. LIFE AS ART IN AMERICA: THE CASE OF MARGARET FULLER. *Studies in the Am. Renaissance 1981: 1-26.*

Traces the development of Margaret Fuller's aesthetic views and personal philosophy, focusing on the impact of her early life in New England on her outlook. From 1810 to 1833 Fuller lived in Cambridge, Massachusetts. She then stayed with her family on a farm in Groton, Connecticut, until 1835, when her principal residence became Boston, and she first became friends with Emerson and other transcendentalists. The cause of Fuller's peculiar response to art and subsequent intellectual and personal eccentricities lies in the cultural poverty and provincialism of the years up to 1846, when she traveled to Europe and finally discovered a continent whose cultural and social consciousness matched her intellectual upbringing and aspirations.

FULLER, META VAUX WARRICK

143. Hoover, Velma J. META VAUX WARRICK FULLER: HER LIFE AND HER ART. *Negro Hist. Bulletin 1977 40(2): 678-681.*

Evaluates the career of the black sculptor Meta Vaux Warrick Fuller (1877-1968). After study in Philadelphia, she went to Paris where her work was highly acclaimed and attracted the favorable attention of Rodin. Back in the United States she received several important commissions, but her powerful sculpture, depicting the sorrows and sufferings of Negroes, was not generally accepted. She turned to portraiture and religious pieces, withdrew into marriage and family life, and at her death was ignored by the art world.

G

GERRY, ELOISE

144. McBeath, Lida W. ELOISE GERRY, A WOMAN OF FOREST SCIENCE. *J. of Forest Hist. 1978 22(3): 128-135.*

Eloise Gerry left her native New England in 1910 to begin a 44-year career as a wood microscopist at the Forest Products Laboratory, Madison, Wisconsin. One of the first women in the country to specialize in forest products research, her achievements as a wood technologist earned her respect and distinction. Her fieldwork in the South, for example, beginning in 1916, contributed to revitalization of the naval stores industry and led as well to a Ph.D. degree at the University of Wisconsin. Gerry engaged in war-related research during the two world wars and also became a leading authority on the habitats and properties of foreign woods. The author of more than 120 publications, she retired from the Forest Service in 1954.

GILMAN, CATHERYNE COOKE

145. Gilman, Elizabeth. CATHERYNE COOKE GILMAN: SOCIAL WORKER.
Stuhler, Barbara and Kreuter, Gretchen, ed.
Women of Minnesota: Selected Biographical Essays (St. Paul: Minnesota Historical Society Press, 1977): 190-207.

Noted teacher, social worker, and feminist Catheryne Cooke Gilman was born in 1880 in the small Missouri town of Laclede. After her high school graduation in 1898, Catheryne Cooke taught social studies in Iowa and, in 1904, became a principal. Subsequently, she attended Iowa State Normal School and did graduate work at the University of Chicago where she discovered new theories, social thought, and social problems. A course by Sophonisba P. Breckinridge introduced Catheryne to feminism and to Jane Addams's Hull House. Cooke took up the new profession of social work, went to New York City's East Side House Settlement, and to the University Settlement directed by Robbins Gilman, whom she married in 1914. They settled in Minneapolis where Robbins conducted the North East Neighborhood House. Catheryne worked as a suffragist, agitated for improved maternity and infant care, and served on the Minnesota Child Welfare Commission. She became a leader of the Women's Co-operative Alliance, organized community studies, and investigated the causes of juvenile delinquency. She promoted sex education and parent-training courses in the schools. During the 1920's and 30's, she campaigned for morality laws and chaired the motion picture committee of the National Congress of Parents and Teachers. From then until her death in 1954, Catheryne Gilman remained at the North East Neighborhood House where she wrote, lectured, and worked.

GILMAN, CHARLOTTE PERKINS

146. Scharnhorst, Gary. MAKING HER FAME: CHARLOTTE PERKINS GILMAN IN CALIFORNIA. *California History 1985 64(3): 192-201.*

Discusses the work of Charlotte Perkins Gilman (1860-1935) as a leader in the Nationalist movement—a socialist movement inspired by Edward Bellamy's novel *Looking Backward.* Married in 1884 but separated from her husband, she was known at the time as Charlotte Perkins Stetson. In 1888, she came to California to pursue a literary career and soon became involved in the Nationalist movement, writing satirical poetry for publication, giving lectures, and correspondin g with Nationalist and socialist leaders. She called for the economic independence of women and for sexual equality. Although the Nationalist movement had foundered by 1895, Gilman continued to pursue a career advocating women's rights that carried the early influence of her California Nationalist experience.

GILMER, ELIZABETH M. (DOROTHY DIX)

147. Culley, Margaret. SOB-SISTERHOOD: DOROTHY DIX AND THE FEMINIST ORIGINS OF THE ADVICE COLUMN. *Southern Studies 1977 16(2): 201-210*

Dorothy Dix (Elizabeth Meriwether Gilmer, 1861-1951), who wrote the first influential and successful newspaper advice column, was an ardent feminist and suffragist. The column began in 1895 in the New Orleans *Picayune* and continued for almost 60 years. Dix later adopted the question and answer format, but in the first six years she wrote strong essays on female financial vulnerability, and the cost to women of confining social conventions and expectations. She supported women's right to work, dress reform, the franchise, improved health care, and education. When she became a nationally syndicated writer, her polemical style softened.

GOLDMAN, EMMA

148. Wexler, Alice. THE EARLY LIFE OF EMMA GOLDMAN. *Psychohistory Rev. 1980 8(4): 7-21.*

Examines the psychological roots of Emma Goldman's career as an anarchist. While Goldman may have rejected her father, she also loved and identified with him. Throughout much of her life she was fascinated with female political martyrs and their lives. This may have influenced her life. Goldman was influenced by her Russian background, making her early history quite different from other Jewish immigrants of the late 19th century. Goldman's psychohistory reveals her anarchism had roots in a desire to separate from her parents and in her need to relieve guilt toward her father and brother. Exposure to strong women early in her life gave Goldman models.

GRAHAM, SHIRLEY

149. Peterson, Bernard L., Jr. SHIRLEY GRAHAM DU BOIS: COMPOSER AND PLAYWRIGHT. *Crisis 1977 84(5): 177-179.*

Shirley Graham Du Bois, widow of William Edward B. Du Bois, was a prolific writer, biographer, composer, and playwright. She composed a three-act music-drama which was later built into the full-scale opera, *Tom-Tom.* She utilized unusual rhythms and instruments, many of which were native to Africa. In 1936 she supervised the Negro Unit of the Chicago Federal Theater. Under a Rosenwald Fellowship, she studied at Yale University, during 1938-40, where she wrote five more plays. Only one play has been published to this date.

GREENFIELD, MARGUERITE

150. Bishop, Joan. GAME OF FREEZE-OUT: MARGUERITE GREENFIELD AND HER BATTLE WITH THE GREAT NORTHERN RAILWAY, 1920-1929. *Montana 1985 35(3): 14-27.*

With her father's assistance, Marguerite Greenfield founded the Independent Ice Company in Helena, Montana, in 1912. Combating community prejudice against women managing ice plants and unfair competition from other ice producers, she managed the ice company in Helena and later in Elk City, Montana, until 1934. Her greatest source of difficulty was the local Great Northern Railway official. She refused his demands for kickbacks in awarding ice contracts, and in return he delayed her shipments, failed to supply adequate rail cars, and generally made her work difficult. After years of complaint, she finally succeeded in getting some relief from the top Great Northern officials.

GUNNESS, BELLE

151. Langlois, Jane L. BELLE GUNNESS, THE LADY BLUEBEARD: SYMBOLIC INVERSION IN VERBAL ART AND AMERICAN CULTURE.
Signs 1983 8(4): 617-634.

Mass murderess Belle Gunness of LaPorte, Indiana, advertised for matrimonial partners to share her farm. She killed each husband with an axe and buried them in her farmyard in unmarked graves. After her death in 1908, Gunness was transformed from a brutal executioner into a tourist attraction and whimsical "Lady Bluebeard," as seen in Ruth Coffeen's 1947 "Ballad of Bloodthirsty Belle." In actuality, Gunness represents the "negative cipher," a legitimate art form in folk culture that humorously represents the contradictions of sexual roles and society's conceptions of them.

H

HALL, JULIA BRAINERD

152. Trescott, Martha Moore. JULIA B. HALL AND ALUMINUM.
Trescott, Martha Moore, ed.
Dynamos and Virgins Revisited: Women and Technological Change in History (Metuchen, N.J.: Scarecrow Pr., 1979): 149-179.

Discusses discrimination against Julia Brainerd Hall (b. 1859), sister of Charles Martin Hall (1863-1914), whose inventions helped found the Pittsburg Reduction Company, forerunner of the Aluminum Company of America. Julia was not recognized for her work by her brother, nor has the significance of her efforts been properly discussed and documented by Charles's biographer and other historians. Julia Hall should be seen as prototypical of many other female relatives of inventors, women who assisted the invention and innovation process in various ways as it took place in or near the home.

HAMILTON, AGNES

153. Carson, Mina J. AGNES HAMILTON OF FORT WAYNE: THE EDUCATION OF A CHRISTIAN SETTLEMENT WORKER. *Indiana Mag. of Hist. 1984 80(1): 1-34.*

Agnes Hamilton became a protege of Jane Addams in the field of settlement work in the late 19th century. Coming from a wealthy Fort Wayne family, she sought to use her formal education as a means of promoting family and Christian values. Exposed to the thinking of such Christian socialist reformers as Charles Kingsley and John Ruskin and the American economist Richard Ely, Miss Hamilton applied her reading by living and serving at Chicago's Hull House. Although she was greatly influenced by Jane Addams's example, Miss Hamilton's work was probably more religiously oriented than that of Addams.

HANCHETT, MARVA CHRISTENSEN

154. Sorenson, Patricia H. THE NURSE: MARVA CHRISTENSEN HANCHETT OF SEVIER COUNTY. *Utah Hist. Q. 1977 45(2): 163-172.*

Marva Christensen Hanchett, after graduating from Salt Lake General Hospital School of Nursing in 1931, was the only registered nurse in Sevier County, Utah. In 1934 she organized the first regular public health program in Sevier County and was its first nurse. From 1957 until retirement in 1974, she supervised public health nursing over one-fifth of the state. A modern nursing pioneer and mother of three children, she successfully combined the careers of nurse and homemaker.

HANSBERRY, LORRAINE

155. Hairston, Loyle. LORRAINE HANSBERRY: PORTRAIT OF AN ANGRY YOUNG WRITER. *Crisis 1979 86(4): 123-128.*

During the early 1950's when the repressive atmosphere had been imposed upon the country by a pervasive phobia of communism, Lorraine Hansberry, a fearless young woman, spoke at popular street-corner rallies on the issues of racism and peace. Born in Chicago on 19 May 1930, her incisive analyses, clarity of understanding, and enthusiasm resulted in her most popular play *Raisin in the Sun.* Her two other artistic triumphs were *Les Blancs* and *The Sign in Brustein's Window.* Her intense involvement in life and her political awareness, nourished by a strong social consciousness imbued her writings with penetrating truths and compelling humanism. On 12 January 1965, at the age of 34, Lorraine Hansberry died of cancer.

HARRIS, EMILY LYLES

156. Racine, Philip N. EMILY LYLES HARRIS: A PIEDMONT FARMER DURING THE CIVIL WAR. *South Atlantic Q. 1980 79(4): 386-397.*

David Harris, a South Carolina farmer eight miles southeast of Spartanburg, began keeping a journal in 1855. When he went off to the Civil War, he encouraged his wife to keep up the journal, which she did. Through her entries we catch a glimpse of what it was like during the Civil War to be the wife of a farmer and a soldier. There is no better contemporary record of daily life in the Spartanburg District and not many its equal for the region. The journal reveals her inmost feelings, especially her depression, which made her feel guilty and incompetent. Her life gave her ample reason to be apprehensive, yet society expected her to react to her burdens otherwise.

HARTSHORN, FLORENCE

157. Mills, Thora McIlroy. MEMORIAL TO THE PACK ANIMALS. *Beaver (Canada) 1980 310(4): 46-51.*

In traveling the 32 miles over the mountains from Skagway, Alaska, to the Klondike on a pony, Florence Hartshorn was "deeply affected . . . [by] the dreadful toll which it took on the pack animals." On her first day in the northland, she vowed "to place a memorial to the[se] animals . . . [which] played such an important part in the extraction of wealth from the gold country." Many details in her life in the Klondike extending over 16 years were extracted from her diary. In 1929, she started a campaign to raise funds for a memorial to the pack animals used on the White Pass Trail. The memorial was unveiled later that year.

HEARST, PHOEBE APPERSON

158. Peterson, Richard H. PHILANTHROPIC PHOEBE: THE EDUCATIONAL CHARITY OF PHOEBE APPERSON HEARST. *California History 1985 64(4): 284-289.*

Profiles Phoebe Apperson Hearst and her philanthropic contributions in support of libraries and public education. Born in Missouri, Phoebe married mining entrepreneur George Hearst in 1862 and moved to California. She became interested in the kindergarten movement, the University of California at Berkeley, public libraries, and other educational institutions, and over the course of her life donated millions of dollars to them. Her interest in helping others was a lifelong and sincere commitment, with immeasurable benefits to education at all levels.

HICKOK, LORENA A.

159. Beasley, Maurine. LORENA HICKOK TO HARRY HOPKINS, 1933: A WOMAN REPORTER VIEWS PRAIRIE HARD TIMES. *Montana 1982 32(2): 58-66.*

Reporter Lorena A. Hickok, the chief investigator for the Federal Emergency Relief Administration (FERA), toured rural Minnesota, North and South Dakota, Nebraska, and Iowa during 1933. She wrote regularly to Eleanor Roosevelt and FERA chief, Harry Hopkins, on the agricultural, economic, social, and political situations she observed. Excerpts from the reports are reprinted along with biographical information on Hickok.

HOWORTH, LUCY SOMERVILLE

160. Hawks, Joanne Varner. LIKE MOTHER, LIKE DAUGHTER: NELLIE NUGENT SOMERVILLE AND LUCY SOMERVILLE HOWORTH. *J. of Mississippi Hist. 1983 45(2): 116-128.*

An overview of the lives of two Mississippi women who served in the state legislature. Nellie Somerville, the first woman elected to the Mississippi legislature, entered public service in 1923 as representative from Washington County through her earlier interests in the temperance and suffrage movements. She worked continuously to involve women in civic improvement projects and other responsibilities of citizenship. Howorth, the daughter, was elected as a state representative from Hinds County in 1931, but her influence would spread beyond the state's boundaries. Appointed initially to the Board of Veterans' Appeals by President Franklin D. Roosevelt, she became an influential part of the network of women in the federal government who were appointed by Roosevelt in the early years of the New Deal. Returning to Mississippi in 1957, she remains active in public life.

HURFORD, GRACE GIBBERD

161. Hurford, Grace Gibberd. MISSIONARY SERVICE IN CHINA. *J. of the Can. Church Hist. Soc. (Canada) 1977 19(3-4): 177-181.*

A personal recollection by a Canadian missionary-educator in China. During her years of service she was a nurse, English instructor, and Christian teacher. Her work offered many rewarding experiences, but from 1937 on she and her fellow workers had to contend with the problems caused by the Japanese invasion. She was injured only once by Japanese bombs, but the danger was omnipresent. Consequently, her work in China was disrupted by the necessity to move on several occasions and by the orders of the Chinese government to close all schools. Her service in China ended with the conclusion of World War II.

HUTCHINSON, ANNE

162. Maclear, J. F. ANNE HUTCHINSON AND THE MORTALIST HERESY. *New England Q. 1981 54(1): 74-103.*

Modern historians of the Antinomian controversy and Anne Hutchinson's 1638 ecclesiastical trial in Massachusetts Bay have ignored Anne's mortalism. The "Soul Sleepers" or mortalists, including Hutchinson, rejected the belief in the conscious immortality of the soul and instead asserted that bodies and souls perish together at death. Hutchinson's belief was both part of the historic Reformation and harbinger of that religious experimentation that characterized many interregnum Puritans. The episode was significant in Puritan history. It shows that the disappearance of mortalism was not quite as total as John Winthrop asserted, clarifies Hutchinson's personality and the nature of her threat to the infant colony, and makes her skepticism about the soul's immortality comprehensible within the context of Continental sectarianism, Stuart Puritanism, and 17th-century intellectual history.

I

IRWIN, HARRIET MORRISON

163. Heisner, Beverly. HARRIET MORRISON IRWIN'S HEXAGONAL HOUSE: AN INVENTION TO IMPROVE DOMESTIC DWELLINGS. *North Carolina Hist. Rev. 1981 58(2): 105-123.*

Harriet Morrison Irwin (1828-97) of Charlotte, North Carolina, was the first woman in the United States to patent an architectural design. Irwin's hexagonal house plan, patented in 1869, expressed her desire for an efficient but open home, with easy access to nature. Her novel, *The Hermit of Petraea* (1871), dedicated to the English writer, John Ruskin, author of popular books on architecture, contains discussions of Irwin's views on the relationship between humans, their homes, and the natural environment. Irwin's own needs as an invalid also influenced her architectural designs. James Patton Irwin (1820-1903), Harriet's husband, advertised her designs in regional magazines. Several homes may have been built according to her designs.

J

JACKSON, HELEN HUNT

164, Marsden, Michael T. A DEDICATION TO THE MEMORY OF HELEN HUNT JACKSON, 1830-1885. *Arizona and the West 1979 21(2): 108-112.*

Helen Maria Fiske Hunt Jackson (1830-85) was a prolific and anonymous writer of children's stories, travel sketches, and magazine essays. An 1879 lecture by two Ponca Indians gave her the consuming passion of her life. She began immediately to compile material on Indian mistreatment and to write tracts, newspaper articles, and petitions at a feverish pace. Her *A Century of Dishonor* submitted massive evidence that the government was dishonest and cruel toward the Indian. Some credit the book with inspiring formation of the Indian Rights Association a year later and with leading to the Dawes Act in 1887. It continues to contribute to the romanticization of the Indian.

JACKSON, MARY PERCY

165. Keywan, Zonia. MARY PERCY JACKSON: PIONEER DOCTOR.
Beaver (Canada) 1977 308(3): 41-47.

In 1929, Dr. Mary Percy left England to practice medicine in northern Alberta. She began near Manning, among new immigrants from Eastern Europe who knew little English. After her marriage to Frank Jackson, they moved to the farm near Keg River. Most of her service here was with local Indians and Metis. With few medical supplies, inadequate transportation, and rarely any income from patients, she continued to provide medical service to the local population until her retirement in 1974. In the past few decades she has become a nationally known spokeswoman for Indian and Metis causes.

JADERBORG, ELIZABETH

166. Jaderborg, Elizabeth. "SELMA LIND" AND LINDSBORG.
Swedish Pioneer Hist. Q. 1980 31(2): 129-133.

"Selma Lind" was the pseudonym of the author when she wrote for the *Lindsborg News-Record* in Kansas during the 1960's. She was born and raised in New England, married a Kansas Swede in 1946, and moved to Lindsborg. Because young people did not know of their rich heritage, she wrote articles on Swedes and the area, based on deductions made through interviews, and some books. As a result of the material written and the interest it generated, "a deluge of background material [came] into the community and its surrounding satellites to prepare them immediately for a centennial celebration."

JOHNSON, EDITH

167. Casey, Naomi Taylor. MISS EDITH JOHNSON: PIONEER NEWSPAPER WOMAN.
Chronicles of Oklahoma 1982 60(1): 66-73.

Edith Johnson began her 50-year newspaper career in 1908 when she was hired as a reporter for the *Daily Oklahoman*. Within 10 years she had passed the stages of beat reporting to writing her own column. The Republic Syndicate eventually carried her Sunday advice column to a host of newspapers throughout the nation. As a champion of the expanding roles of women, she published *Women of the Business World* in 1923 and used her column to encourage women into enterprises previously reserved for men.

JOHNSON, SONIA HARRIS

168. Bradford, Mary L. THE ODYSSEY OF SONIA JOHNSON.
Dialogue 1981 14(2): 14-26.

Overviews the life of Sonia Harris Johnson during 1936-81, her childhood and youth in northern Utah, early experiences as a Mormon, graduation from Utah State University, and marriage to Richard Johnson. Discusses the couple's frequent relocations due to his career goals, the birth of their children, and the Johnsons' eventual divorce. Extensive coverage is given to her confrontation with the leaders of Mormonism over the Equal Rights Amendment. In 1979 Sonia Johnson was excommunicated from the church for her public criticism of Mormonism.

K

KASSING, EDITH FORCE

169. Tomer, John S. EDITH FORCE KASSING: SCIENTIST WITH A GIFT FOR TEACHING.
Chronicles of Oklahoma 1985-86 63(4): 396-411.

Edith Force Kassing (1890-1966) earned a national reputation as a researcher in Oklahoma ornithology and herpetology. While a teacher at Tulsa's Woodrow Wilson Junior High School from 1926 to 1956, she organized a Junior Academy of Science chapter and the Field and Stream Club, which participated in many field trips and collected thousands of specimens. Many of these specimens went to illustrious institutions, such as the Oklahoma State University Museum, the University of Oklahoma Museum of Zoology, the University of Tulsa, the National Museum of Natural History, and the US Biological Survey in Washington, D.C. Kassing alsoreceived honors from the Oklahoma Academy of Science and other research organizations for her scores of published articles.

KELLER, HELEN

170. Giffin, Frederick C. THE RADICAL VISION OF HELEN KELLER. *Int. Social Sci. Rev. 1984 59(4): 27-32.*

Helen Keller was an active participant in the American radical movement. A member of the Socialist Party, she was particularly outspoken in her opposition to World War I, a conflict she identified as a "capitalistic war" which in no sense served the interests of the working class. After the United States joined the struggle in April 1917, Keller was an impassioned supporter of Emma Goldman, Eugene Debs, and other radicals sent to prison as a result of their antiwar activities.

KELLEY, FLORENCE

171. Harmon, Sandra D. FLORENCE KELLEY IN ILLINOIS. *J. of the Illinois State Hist. Soc. 1981 74(3): 162-178.*

Florence Kelley was a major force in the struggle for protection of laboring children and women throughout her career as a resident of Hull House, the first Illinois factory inspector, and general secretary of the National Consumers' League. A graduate of Cornell University, she was introduced to socialism at the University of Zurich. The abuses of sweatshops led Governor John P. Altgeld to appoint her factory inspector on 12 July 1893. She exposed widespread illiteracy, poor hygiene, and unsafe working conditions. Her work relied on the use of trained inspectors, collection of reliable statistics, issuance of public reports, and legislative lobbying.

L

LANGTRY, LILLIE

172. Herr, Pamela. LILLIE ON THE FRONTIER:
WESTERN ADVENTURES OF A FAMOUS BEAUTY.
Am. West 1981 18(2): 40-45.

Bewitching Lillie Langtry (b. 1853) dazzled Victorian England.
She was a mistress of the Prince of Wales for a few years.
Turning to the stage for a career, she earned success and
notoriety in Great Britain and the United States. She became the
highest-paid performer in American theatrical history, took out
American citizenship, lived on a California ranch, made several
western tours, and again took up residence in England. Among
many others, Judge Roy Bean, self-styled "law west of the
Pecos," was smitten with her beauty (from a magazine picture).
In 1884, he changed the name of Vinegarroon, Texas, to
Langtry, but he died several months before she honored the
town with a visit in 1904.

LARSON, AGNES, HENRIETTA, AND NORA

173. Jenson, Carol. THE LARSON SISTERS: THREE
CAREERS IN CONTRAST.
Stuhler, Barbara and Kreuter, Gretchen, ed.
*Women of Minnesota: Selected Biographical Essays (St. Paul:
Minnesota Historical Society Press, 1977): 301-324.*

Agnes, Henrietta, and Nora Larson grew up in Minnesota.
Daughters of a successful farmer-businessman and a gentle
mother, they were raised in an environment of Norwegian
American traditions and the Lutheran Church. They all attended
St. Olaf College in Northfield, pursued graduate studies, and
became teachers. Agnes Larson became a historian, taught at St.
Olaf, and wrote the meticulously researched and well-written
monograph, *History of the White Pine Industry* in Minnesota.
Henrietta Larson became a prominent pioneer in business
history. She taught at colleges and universities. She became a
noted editor and writer while working as a research associate at
Harvard, where she became the first woman named as an
associate professor by the business school despite that

university's tradition of sex discrimination. Nora Larson became a bacteriologist. She did research at the Mayo Foundation, the Lakey Clinic, and the Takamine Laboratories before finally settling back in Minnesota in 1950, where she became the only woman among the principal scientists at the University of Minnesota's Hormel Institute. She studied swine diseases and was active in professional and community organizations. In 1960, Nora joined the faculty of St. Olaf where she taught until her retirement in 1972.

LEASE, MARY ELIZABETH

174. Blumberg, Dorothy Rose. MARY ELIZABETH LEASE, POPULIST ORATOR: A PROFILE. *Kansas Hist. 1978 1(1): 1-15.*

Mary Elizabeth Lease (1850-1933), long identified as a principal spokesman for Kansas Populism, emerges as a determined champion of many causes. Seldom a political theorist, Mrs. Lease was an effective political advocate. Her speeches and writings articulated the plight of farmers, urban workers, and women struggling for rights in a world run by men.

LINCOLN, MARY TODD

175. Sklar, Kathryn Kish. VICTORIAN WOMEN AND DOMESTIC LIFE: MARY TODD LINCOLN, ELIZABETH CADY STANTON, AND HARRIET BEECHER STOWE. Davis, Cullom; Strozier, Charles B.; Veach, Rebecca Monroe; and Ward, Geoffrey C., ed. *The Public and the Private Lincoln: Contemporary Perspectives (Carbondale: So. Illinois U. Pr., 1979): 20-37.*

Examines efforts by prominent Victorian women to limit the size of their families and their public and private activities to arrive at a qualitative rather than quantitative definition of motherhood, during 1830-80. Harriet Beecher Stowe's strategy was to abstain from sex, in part to punish her philandering husband, undertake a literary career, and foster women's education. Elizabeth Cady Stanton, like Stowe, practiced family planning and worked for feminist domestic reform, seeking the legal equality of women. Mary Todd Lincoln's approach was total commitment to her husband and children. In part she practiced family planning to aid her husband's political career, and she was indulgent of her children. She did not separate domestic from public life, participating in the political sector on Abraham's behalf, but she was unable to build an autonomous career.

LOPP, ELLEN KITTREDGE

176. Engerman, Jeanne. LETTERS FROM CAPE PRINCE OF WALES. A MISSION FAMILY IN NORTHWESTERN ALASKA 1892-1902. *Alaska Journal 1984 14(4): 33-41.*

Describes the Alaska life of missionary Ellen Kittredge Lopp, who taught with her husband W. T. "Tom" Lopp in the government school at isolated Cape Prince of Wales, Alaska. Icebound nine months a year, Ellen Lopp wrote hundreds of letters to family and friends describing the everyday life at the mission. Besides teaching and preaching to the Eskimos there were the six children she bore to be cared for. Her letters reveal a powerful belief in her work however, and even after 10 years at the outpost, she had a strong reluctance to leave.

LOW, JULIETTE GORDON

177. Strickland, Charles E. JULIETTE LOW, THE GIRL SCOUTS, AND THE ROLE OF AMERICAN WOMEN. Kelley, Mary, ed. *Woman's Being, Woman's Place: Female Identity and Vocation in American History (Boston: G. K. Hall, 1979): 252-264.*

Employing Erik Erikson's life-cycle model, records a convergence of personal and historical crises in the life of Juliette Low (b. 1860), founder of the Girl Scouts of America. Prepared to assume the role of companion, hostess, and mother of children, Low instead faced loneliness, confronted a childless existence, and ran headlong into her husband's affair with a widow. The result was a marriage that not only brought anguish but ended in a humiliating divorce. Alone and unable to find an alternative role, Low considered her life devoid of meaning. Her opportunity to resolve her crisis of identity came only when she found in the Girl Scout movement a cause to which she could dedicate herself. Scouting might not have challenged all conventional definitions of women's role and sphere, but under Low's tutelage it did demand that women become more than delicate, helpless ornaments.

M

MACLANE, MARY

178. Mattern, Carolyn J. MARY MAC LANE: A FEMINIST OPINION. *Montana 1977 27(4): 54-63.*

Mary MacLane (1881-1929) wrote three books—*The Story of Mary MacLane* (1902), *My Friend Annabel Lee* (1903), and *I, Mary MacLane* (1917)—authored numerous articles, then wrote and starred in a movie, *Men Who Have Made Love To Me* (1917). Her activities created a sensation in her hometown of Butte, Montana, and nationwide. Although at ypical, she was not an eccentric woman. Her ideas arose and developed from her environment, reflected the mainstream of feminist thought, and represented ideas or feelings of educated, middle class women during that era. An unhappy, self-centered young woman, MacLane craved understanding and self-expression, believing all women should be free to live fully expressive lives. During 1902-10, MacLane found happiness in the intellectual bohemia of New York City's Greenwich Village and had several affairs with men, viewing the associations dispassionately. After her return to Butte in 1910, and a near fatal bout with scarlet fever, MacLane's writing evidenced a sense of life's fragility and her own mortality; she died lonely and forgotten in Chicago.

MARY JOSEPH, MOTHER

179. McKernan, Mary. MOTHER JOSEPH: PIONEER NUN. *Am. West 1981 18(5): 20-21.*

Esther Pariseau (1823-1902), who learned carpentry from her father, a Canadian carriage maker, entered the Montreal, Quebec, convent of the Sisters of Charity of Providence and soon became Mother Mary Joseph. In 1856, she was assigned to duty in the Pacific Northwest. She constructed (literally as "fund raiser, architect, estimator of materials, supervisor of construction, and at times as carpenter, bricklayer, and wood-carver") 11 hospitals, seven academies, two orphanages, four homes for the aged and mentally ill, and five Indian schools. She wore a hammer beside the rosary on her belt. Most of her recognition has come posthumously from the American Institute of Architects, the National Register of Historic Places, and the state of Washington, which chose her as its second representative in Statuary Hall at the nation's Capitol.

MAYO, MARY A. BRYANT

180. Marti, Donald B. WOMAN'S WORK IN THE GRANGE: MARY ANN MAYO OF MICHIGAN, 1882-1903. *Agric. Hist. 1982 56(2): 439-452.*

The Grange gave new opportunities for farm women to develop personally, though generally in ways related to the traditional spheres of home and family. Mary Ann Mayo became active as a Grange lecturer in Michigan, urging women to widen their cultural horizons and take a moral and scientific approach to housework. She argued for domestic science courses in the state's agricultural college and was active with a variety of charities, especially a project to give poor city children the opportunity to stay on a farm. Mayo became the most important women's Grange leader in Michigan.

MCDONALD, ALICE

181. McDonald, Alice. AS WELL AS ANY MAN. *Alaska Journal 1984 14(3): 39-45.*

Presents an autobiographical account of the labors of Alice McDonald, a Swedish woman who went to seek her fortune in Alaskan mining camps. She worked as a cook in Dawson for a time, then did odd jobs, such as blueberry picking, baking, and laundering while her husband prospected for gold. She opened a hotel in Iditarod and, when business dwindled, moved to California, where she began writing her memoirs at age 84.

MCDOUGAL, MYRTLE ARCHER

182. Hoder-Salmon, Marilyn. MYRTLE ARCHER MCDOUGAL: LEADER OF OKLAHOMA'S "TIMID SISTERS."
Chronicles of Oklahoma 1982 60(3): 332-343.

Myrtle Archer McDougal joined her attorney husband in Sapulpa during 1904 and within a decade rose to prominence in Oklahoma suffrage, health reform, and women's club movements. Armed with a powerful oratorical style, she promoted reform in women's dress styles; pensions for widowed, abandoned, and divorced mothers; a rural library movement; and a national prohibition crusade. Oil wealth allowed McDougal to pursue these causes almost full time after 1908, and during the following 20 years she served on nationally prestigious committees for the Democratic Party.

MCLEAN, MARY HANCOCK

183. Hunt, Marion. WOMAN'S PLACE IN MEDICINE: THE CAREER OF DR. MARY HANCOCK MCLEAN.
Missouri Hist. Soc. Bulletin 1980 36(4): 255-263.

Though her behavior defied social conventions, Mary Hancock McLean (1861-1930) was able to become a physician and surgeon in 1883. Medical education was then available to women so that, trained, they might medically attend to other women and children. Despite obstacles, she proved to the St. Louis medical fraternity that female physicians deserved a larger sphere than was traditionally granted them.

MCVICKER, EMMA J.

184. Lubomudrov, Carol Ann. A WOMAN STATE SCHOOL SUPERINTENDENT: WHATEVER HAPPENED TO MRS. MCVICKER?
Utah Hist. Q. 1981 49(3): 254-261.

Emma J. McVicker was appointed by Governor Heber M. Wells to be Utah's second state school superintendent on 8 October

1900. In 1896 she had been the first woman regent of the University of Utah. Prior to this time she had served as administrator of free kindergarten schools. While state superintendent, she observed many schools, urged reforms in the teaching of young children, criticized demeanor of male teachers, and urged better health education. Her superintendent's report of 1900 is the only extant record of her work and goals.

MEAD, MARGARET

185. Mabee, Carleton. MARGARET MEAD AND A "PILOT EXPERIMENT" IN PROGRESSIVE AND INTERRACIAL EDUCATION: THE DOWNTOWN COMMUNITY SCHOOL. *New York Hist. 1984 65(1): 4-31.*

By the time her daughter had reached school age in 1945, Margaret Mead had become famous as an anthropologist and advocate of progressive education. Mead decided to enroll her daughter in the newly established Downtown Community School in New York City. The school soon became well known for its interracial and progressive practices. Although Mead withdrew her daughter from the school in 1950, her interest in interracial and intercultural education continued and, by the 1970's, she had come to realize that education was not a "one way process" but circular, with all contributing and profiting from the experience.

MERIWETHER, ELIZABETH AVERY

186. Berkeley, Kathleen Christine. ELIZABETH AVERY MERIWETHER, "AN ADVOCATE FOR HER SEX": FEMINISM AND CONSERVATISM IN THE POST-CIVIL WAR SOUTH. *Tennessee Historical Quarterly 1984 43(4): 390-407.*

Elizabeth Avery Meriwether, unlike her famous contemporary, Mary Chesnut, was willing to challenge Southern politics and society publicly and to militate for social reform. After the Civil War, while her husband was helping establish the Ku Klux Klan in Tennessee, she became a temperance and women's rights activist by writing about the legal discrimination suffered by women in Tennessee and by waging an assault on "that aspect of common law, coverture, which subjected married women to the control of their husbands." In 1873, she tried to convince the Tennessee legislature to grant female teachers equal pay for equal work, and she joined with suffragettes such as Susan B. Anthony to press for a federal woman suffrage amendment.

MILLER, ANNE FITZHUGH

187. Huff, Robert A. ANNE MILLER AND THE GENEVA POLITICAL EQUALITY CLUB, 1897-1912. *New York History 1984 65(4): 324-348.*

Among the many reform-minded people who lived and worked in western New York during the 19th and early 20th centuries were Elizabeth Smith Miller and her daughter, Anne Fitzhugh Miller. Elizabeth, daughter of Gerrit Smith and cousin of Elizabeth Cady Stanton, was well known by the time the family moved to Geneva in 1869. By the 1890's, Anne had also become active in reform causes, especially the suffrage movement. Both mother and daughter also were interested in spiritualism. Anne was instrumental in forming the Geneva Political Equality Club, of which Elizabeth was honorary president until her death in 1911. The influence of the club was widespread over the next decade and continued to be an important factor in the suffrage movement until New York passed its equal suffrage amendment in 1917. Anne, however, did not live to see its ultimate success; she died suddenly in 1912.

MOHRBACHER, ELLEN WHITMORE

188. Pieroth, Doris Hinson. THE ONLY SHOW IN TOWN: ELLEN WHITMORE MOHRBACHER'S SAVOY THEATRE. *Chronicles of Oklahoma 1982 60(3): 260-279.*

A daughter of Oklahoma pioneers, Ellen Whitmore Mohrbacher raised a family and maintained a flourishing movie theater business following her husband's death in 1918. She purchased the failing Savoy Theatre in Prague, Oklahoma, during 1921 and transformed it into a regal entertainment center, complete with all the latest equipment and movies. Mohrbacher personally booked all films and refused those she considered to be of questionable moral value. In 1943, her theater hosted the world premier of *Hangmen Also Die*. Business gradually declined in the 1950's due to competition from television, and the theater was sold in 1958.

MOLLOY, MARY ALOYSIUS

189. Kennelly, Karen. MARY MOLLOY: WOMEN'S COLLEGE FOUNDER.
Stuhler, Barbara and Kreuter, Gretchen, ed.
Women of Minnesota: Selected Biographical Essays (St. Paul: Minnesota Historical Society Press, 1977): 116-135.

Born on 14 June 1880, in Sandusky, Ohio, Mary Aloysia Molloy grew up as the only child of Irish Catholic immigrant parents. In an age when few women attended college, Molloy earned her way through Ohio State University and graduated, in 1903, with more honors than anyone else up to that time. She went on to earn a master's degree and election to Phi Beta Kappa at Ohio State. In 1907 she earned her doctorate at Cornell. That same year, she began her career as a Catholic college educator in Winona, Minnesota, when she accepted a job with the Franciscan Sisters who, under the leadership of Sister Leo Tracy, were creating the liberal arts College of St. Teresa. The two women persevered and successfully established and administered the new collegiate institution for Catholic lay and religious women. Molloy was unique as the lay dean of a Catholic college, but in 1922 she became a nun, Sister Mary Aloysius Molloy, and in 1928 became the college president. As an educator, Molloy worked hard to improve the quality of women's education, wrestled with the unique problems of Catholic colleges, and carefully oversaw the development of her own school. By 1946, when she retired, the college was a firmly established institution producing outstanding graduate women. One of the last among the heroic generation of founders of Minnesota women's colleges, Molloy died on 27 September 1954.

MORTON, ELIZABETH HOMER

190. Bassam, Bertha. ELIZABETH HOMER MORTON: LIBRARIAN, ADMINISTRATOR, AUTHOR, EDITOR . . . *Can. Lib. J. (Canada) 1978 35(4): 253-267.*

Reviews the contributions of Elizabeth Homer Morton, who served from 1946 to 1968 as executive director of the Canadian Library Association and chief editor of the *Canadian Library Journal.* In those positions, she helped establish the National Library of Canada and the *Canadian Periodical Index.* From 1944 to 1946, she had served as secretary of both the Canadian Library Council (the predecessor of the Canadian Library Association) and the Ontario Library Association, while employed by the Toronto Public Library. She finished a Master of Arts program at the graduate Library School of the University of Chicago upon retirement, and opened a library consulting firm.

MUSSER, ELISE FURER

191. Brooks, Juanita, ed., and Butler, Janet G., ed. UTAH'S PEACE ADVOCATE, THE "MORMONA": ELISE FURER MUSSER.
Utah Hist. Q. 1978 46(2): 151-166.

Excerpts the writings, diaries, and letters of Elise Furer Musser (1877-1967), who was born in Switzerland, migrated to Utah in 1897, and married Burton Musser in 1911. Her social service and political career began with work in Neighborhood House. She became influential in Utah's Democratic Women's Club, serving as state senator (1933-34), and was the only woman delegate to the Buenos Aires Peace Conference in 1936. Her life puts the current women's liberation movement into perspective as a continuum rather than a new, spontaneous phenomenon.

MYERS, RUTH IOWA JONES

192. Hickle, Evelyn Myers. RUTH IOWA JONES MYERS, 1887-1974: RURAL IOWA EDUCATOR.
Ann. of Iowa 1980 45(3): 196-211.

Throughout much of her adult life, Ruth Iowa Jones Myers served as a rural educator. First as a teacher in a one-room country school, then as a 4-H Club leader, a participant in the Country Life Association, and later as a part-time employee of the Agricultural Adjustment Administration, she sought to improve the lives of children and adults in the rural community.

N

NATION, CARRY AMELIA

193. Blochowiak, Mary Ann. "WOMAN WITH A HATCHETT": CARRY NATION COMES TO OKLAHOMA TERRITORY. *Chronicles of Oklahoma 1981 59(2): 132-151.*

Carry Nation entered the temperance crusade following her 1867 marriage to Charles Gloyd, a hopeless alcoholic. A second marriage led her to Richmond, Texas, where she underwent a religious awakening that fired her crusading enthusiasm. In 1899 she launched her famous "hatchet campaigns" against saloons in Kansas and Oklahoma. Nation's militancy caused various chapters of the Women's Christian Temperance Union to close their doors to her, and she responded to them with venom. Local sheriffs frequently arrested Carry Nation and her following subsided by 1906. She died alone and penniless at Leavenworth, Kansas, in 1911.

NELSON, JULIA BULLARD

194. Lief, Julia Wiech. A WOMAN OF PURPOSE: JULIA B. NELSON. *Minnesota Hist. 1981 47(8): 302-314.*

Julia Bullard Nelson, widowed at 26 in 1869, spent the next 19 years teaching in black schools in Texas and Tennessee, the last three years of which she acted as principal of the Warner Institute. Returning to Minnesota in 1888 she labored in turn as a Women's Christian Temperance Union (WCTU) organizer, a National Woman Suffrage Association lecturer and then editor of the state WCTU monthly paper. Also active in local affairs in

Red Wing, she was the Populist candidate for superintendent of schools in 1896. Her will capped an unconventional life by bequeathing much of her estate to a former black pupil.

NORTON, MARY T.

195. Mitchell, Gary. WOMEN STANDING FOR WOMEN: THE EARLY POLITICAL CAREER OF MARY T. NORTON. *New Jersey Hist. 1978 96(1-2): 27-42.*

Before her election to Congress in 1924 as a representative from Frank Hague's Hudson County, Mary T. Norton worked with working class women in Jersey City, New Jersey, organized women for the Democratic Party, served on New Jersey's Democratic State Committee, and became a county freeholder. During her early congressional career she introduced legislation designed to help women achieve equality on the District of Columbia's police force and on its juries. She spoke out on immigration equalization for women and introduced legislation to increase pensions for Civil War veteran's widows. Norton fought throughout her career to be judged by her record, not her sex. She urged women everywhere to become involved in politics.

NOTESTEIN, ADA COMSTOCK

196. Smith, Susan Margot. ADA COMSTOCK NOTESTEIN, EDUCATOR. Stuhler, Barbara and Kreuter, Gretchen, ed. *Women of Minnesota: Selected Biographical Essays (St. Paul: Minnesota Historical Society Press, 1977): 208-225.*

Ada Comstock Notestein (1876-1973) was an intelligent, resourceful young woman. She attended the University of Minnesota, Smith College, and Columbia University. In 1899, she accepted a fellowship at the University of Minnesota and began her long, distinguished career as an educator. In 1907, she became the first dean of women at the University of Minnesota; in 1912, she became Dean of Smith College. In 1923 she became the first full-time president of Radcliffe College. In all these positions, her concern for and leadership in quality education for women were manifest. In 1943, she retired as

Radcliffe's president, married historian Wallace Notestein, and combined marriage with her academic interest. She remained active in the affairs of Smith and Radcliffe and in other educational matters.

O

O'BRIEN, ALICE

197. Michels, Eileen Manning. ALICE O'BRIEN: VOLUNTEER AND PHILANTHROPIST. Stuhler, Barbara and Kreuter, Gretchen, ed. *Women of Minnesota: Selected Biographical Essays (St. Paul: Minnesota Historical Society Press, 1977): 136-154.*

Alice O'Brien was born on 1 September 1891 in the affluent Summit Hill area of St. Paul. The daughter of a wealthy lumberman, Alice attended private schools, traveled extensively, and became a prominent philanthropist and art collector. A curious, intelligent, and self-directed individual, Alice O'Brien was part of a large, affectionate, Irish Catholic family. She spent World War I as a volunteer mechanic, nurse, and canteen worker in Europe. She helped make a documentary film of Africa during the 1920's. Thereafter, she returned to St. Paul and participated in many social and political affairs, including the National Prohibition Reform movement and Wendell Willkie's presidential campaign. Her two major interests were the Women's City Club and the Children's Hospital, to which she devoted much time, energy, and money. During her later years, O'Brien continued to financially help many civic organizations. She established the Alice M. O'Brien Foundation to support educational, scientific, religious, and charitable causes; and she became interested in conservation, especially in Florida where she spent many winters. She was on her way to Florida in November 1962 when she died.

OTIS, ELIZA ANN

198. Sherwood, Midge. ELIZA ANN OTIS, CO-FOUNDER OF THE LOS ANGELES TIMES. *Pacific Hist. 1984 28(3): 45-53.*

Strives to portray accurately the life and times of Eliza Ann Otis, whose accomplishments have been overshadowed by those of her more illustrious husband, General Harrison Gray Otis, the legendary publisher of the Los Angeles *Times*. Although she has received little recognition as a journalist, Eliza Otis played an important role on the newspaper. In addition to writing a couple of regular columns, "she was also in charge of the religion, society, fashion, literature, drama, and "women's section"' of the *Times* during the 1880's-90's.

P

PACKARD, ELIZABETH

199. Himelhoch, Myra Samuels and Shaffer, Arthur H. ELIZABETH PACKARD: NINETEENTH-CENTURY CRUSADER FOR THE RIGHTS OF MENTAL PATIENTS. *J. of Am. Studies (Great Britain) 1979 13(3): 343-375.*

Presentation of dubious evidence of insanity resulted in a three-year confinement for Elizabeth Packard (1816-97) in the Illinois State Hospital. Released in 1863, she crusaded successfully during the next 30 years for statutes which could prevent injustices within the asylums. To achieve this reform, she attacked physicians who traditionally determined mental competency, and she criticized their methods of treating asylum patients. Consequently, she was publicly maligned throughout the remainder of her lifetime. Not until the 1930's did scholars begin to acknowledge her reform achievements.

PATTERSON, MARGARET NORRIS

200. Gordon, Loraine. DOCTOR MARGARET NORRIS PATTERSON: FIRST WOMAN POLICE MAGISTRATE IN EASTERN CANADA—TORONTO—JANUARY 1922 TO NOVEMBER 1934. *Atlantis (Canada) 1984 10(1): 95-109.*

Summarizes the career of Toronto's Dr. Margaret Norris Patterson, who from 1922 to 1934 served as the first woman police magistrate in eastern Canada. Patterson's earlier professional career consisted of medical missionary work in India and volunteer social work in Toronto. As a magistrate in Toronto, Patterson dealt with a variety of social problems, including those related to the subordinate status of women in society. Though Patterson often expressed controversial opinions and had a reputation as a strict-sentencing magistrate, she received strong support from public-service groups, if not always from the Canadian government or Toronto newspapers. Patterson lost her position in 1934 as a result of the Hepburn administration's efforts to reduce expenses.

PETERS, LAURA HALL

201. Cloud, Barbara. LAURA HALL PETERS: PURSUING THE MYTH OF EQUALITY. *Pacific Northwest Q. 1983 74(1): 28-36.*

Following her 1883 divorce, Laura Hall became increasingly involved in social reform movements around the Seattle area. In addition to working for women's suffrage, she joined the Knights of Labor and the Populist movement. She also promoted the utopian Puget Sound Co-operative Colony and edited its newspaper, *Model Commonwealth.* Her 1888 marriage to reform-minded Charles J. Peters heightened the crusading instinct which she maintained until her death in 1902.

PHELPS, ALMIRA LINCOLN

202. Scott, Anne Firor. ALMIRA LINCOLN PHELPS: THE SELF-MADE WOMAN IN THE NINETEENTH CENTURY. *Maryland Hist. Mag. 1980 75(3): 203-216.*

Almira Lincoln Phelps (1793-1884) was the archetype of a 19th-century woman who found the essential compromise between the social and familial role demanded of women, and the pursuit of an independent career which challenged contemporary mores. Her teaching in various Massachusetts schools led to her career as head of the Patapsco Female Institute, 1841-65. In her two published volumes of lectures, in a novel, and in numerous essays, she developed for young women the art of self-education and the methods of building an autonomous identity in the face of a firm net of cultural doctrine which assumed women to be merely handmaidens to men.

PHILBROOK, MARY

203. Petrick, Barbara. RIGHT OR PRIVILEGE? THE ADMISSION OF MARY PHILBROOK TO THE BAR. *New Jersey Hist. 1979 97(2): 91-104.*

At age 20, Mary Philbrook was interested in becoming an attorney primarily to make a living. In 1895, by an act of the legislature more than one year after she first sought admittance to the bar, she was given the right to take the qualifying examinations. Because of the attention she received as the first woman lawyer in New Jersey, Mary Philbrook soon became involved with the causes espoused by the women's movement. She acted as a legal counsel, lobbied, and gave speeches on women's rights issues, especially suffrage. One of her last acts was to fight for an equal rights provision in New Jersey's 1947 state constitution.

PICKENS, LUCY HOLCOMBE

204. Bull, Emily L. LUCY PICKENS: FIRST LADY OF THE SOUTH CAROLINA CONFEDERACY. *Pro. of the South Carolina Hist. Assoc. 1982: 5-18.*

Describes the life of Lucy Petway Hunt Holcombe Pickens, who was the wife of the Civil War governor of South Carolina and whose picture appeared on the Confederate $100 bill. Born in LaGrange, Tennessee, of aristocratic background, Lucy Pickens was an educated and popular woman. While her husband was ambassador to Russia, she captivated Russian society, just as she did South Carolina society upon her return. After the Civil War and the death of her husband in 1869, she was active in church and civic affairs until her death in 1899.

PICOTTE, SUSAN LAFLESCHE

205. Mathes, Valerie Sherer. SUSAN LAFLESCHE
PICOTTE: INDIAN PHYSICIAN.
Masterkey 1983 57(1): 10-14.

Daughter of the last Omaha chief and later wife of a Sioux,
Susan LaFlesche was the first Indian woman to graduate from a
medical college and to practice medicine; she helped organize
the county medical association, served on the health board and
as chairman of the health committee for the Nebraska
Federation of Women's Clubs, and lived just long enough to see
her dream hospital built nearby.

R

RANKIN, JEANNETTE

206. Wilson, Joan Hoff. [JEANNETTE RANKIN AND
AMERICAN FOREIGN POLICY].
"PEACE IS A WOMAN'S JOB": JEANNETTE RANKIN AND
AMERICAN FOREIGN POLICY: THE ORIGINS OF HER
PACIFISM.
Montana 1980 30(1): 28-41.

Jeannette Pickering Rankin (1880-1973), of Montana, was the
first woman elected to the US House of Representatives (1916)
and the only member of Congress to have opposed American
entrance into both world wars. The oldest of seven children,
Rankin entered the political world normally reserved for men.
She experienced self-doubt and a sense of inferiority, but
presented a public image of great self-confidence. Pioneer ideals
of hard work, honesty, and perseverance, which she accepted as
a youth, and her perceptions of women, international conflict,
and the destructiveness of war, made Rankin unique in
American political history, as a suffragist and pacifist. Her vote
against war in 1917 influenced her political thinking for the rest
of her life.

JEANNETTE RANKIN AND AMERICAN FOREIGN
POLICY: HER LIFEWORK AS A PACIFIST.
Montana 1980 30(2): 38-53.

From 1917 until her death in 1973, Rankin remained a staunch advocate of domestic reform, peace, neutrality, and disarmament. She worked privately and through such groups as the National Council for the Prevention of War and the Georgia Peace Society. Rankin admired Gandhi's work in India and opposed American involvement in Korea and Vietnam. The meaning of her life and views on foreign policy was more symbolic than practical, representing the generation of American women at the turn of the century who believed in a global society of peace.

RHODES, MARY W. K. D.

207. Pister, M. Claire. MARY. *Pacific Hist. 1980 24(3): 325-343.*

Mary W. K. D. Rhodes (13 October 1808-16 September 1893), the author's great-grandmother, was born and educated in New Hampshire. She was a teacher; when widowed in the 1830's in Charleston, South Carolina, she resumed teaching. In 1838 she married Colonel Elisha Rhodes and moved to Galveston Island, Texas. Her husband was the US Consul to the Republic of Texas. When he was ill or away, she took care of his business. When Colonel Rhodes became an invalid in 1848, Mary took over running the family of his, her, and their children. For financial reasons she went to California alone in 1850, set up a boarding house in San Francisco, and bought some property in Stockton. The family was brought west, where its fortunes went up and down. Mary built Windsor Farm in Stockton. Mary supported the South in the Civil War and lost her two younger sons in that conflict. She left the farm to Stark Blount Smith, Jr., her grandson who had cared for her and the farm.

RICH, HELEN

208. Safanda, Elizabeth M. and Mead, Molly L. THE LADIES OF FRENCH STREET IN BRECKENRIDGE. *Colorado Mag. 1979 56(1-2): 19-34.*

Helen Rich (1894-1972), journalist, and Belle Turnbull (1882-1970), teacher, met in Colorado Springs in 1930 and became fast friends. Together they moved permanently to Summit

County in 1938, eager to concentrate on writing poetry and novels. For some 30 years they lived in a fairly primitive log cabin on French Street in Breckenridge. They explored the area, familiarized themselves with mining technology, and participated in community life. From their experience came several unromanticized novels and many poems documenting with precision the lives of "ordinary" men and women of the mining country for regional historians and students of literature.

RICHARDS, LOUISA LULA GREENE

209. Bennion, Sherilyn Cox. LULA GREENE RICHARDS: UTAH'S FIRST WOMAN EDITOR. *Brigham Young U. Studies 1981 21(2): 155-174.*

Gives a short biographical sketch of Louisa Lula Greene Richards (1849-1944), American Mormon journalist and poet, reporting major events in her career as journal editor and columnist. Her first editorship, at age 20, was with the *Smithfield Sunday School Gazette.* Two years later, the *Salt Lake Daily Herald* offered her an editorship. She was asked to edit a new women's periodical called *The Woman's Exponent.* She was employed six years, then resigned to rear her six children. Six years later, however, she was asked to write a column for *The Juvenile Instructor,* to which she contributed for 24 years. In 1904 she published her first book, *Branches That Run Over the Wall.* For the next 40 years, she was a regular contributor to Mormon publications. Contains excerpts from her poems.

RICHMAN, JULIA

210. Berrol, Selma. WHEN UPTOWN MET DOWNTOWN: JULIA RICHMAN'S WORK IN THE JEWISH COMMUNITY OF NEW YORK, 1880-1912. *Am. Jewish Hist. 1980 70(1): 35-51.*

Traces the career of Julia Richman (1855-1912), first Jewish woman school principal, first Jewish district superintendent of schools, a founder of the Young Women's Hebrew Association and the National Council of Jewish Women, a director of the Hebrew Free School Association and the Educational Alliance, and a lecturer and author for the Jewish Chautauqua Society. As a Progressive reformer, Richman sought to improve secular and Jewish education to achieve a more orderly, ethical, and equitable society. She criticized East European Jewish immigrants as deficient in moral values, and was in turn criticized by them, yet she continued to work on their behalf. Her career illuminates the Progressive Era, the place of women reformers in it, and the relationship between "uptown" and "downtown" in New York City's Jewish community.

RIDGELY, ELIZA EICHELBERGER

211. Shipe, Bess Paterson. ELIZA EICHELBERGER RIDGELY, THE *LADY WITH A HARP*. *Maryland Hist. Mag. 1982 77(3): 230-237.*

Eliza Eichelberger Ridgely (1803-67), the cultivated mistress of Hampton Plantation, epitomized the traditions of Maryland elegance and hospitality. Her home, now maintained by the National Park Service, still contains the imported chandeliers, Italian art, and Turkish carpets brought back by Eliza from her European travels. Her gardens became a showplace of America in the 1840's. Thomas Sully's portrait of Eliza in 1818, the *Lady With a Harp*, is a remarkable memoir of the beautiful Baltimore belle who corresponded with Lafayette for 10 years and went on to become a symbol of the sophisticated life of antebellum Maryland.

ROBB, ISABEL HAMPTON

212. James, Janet Wilson. ISABEL HAMPTON AND THE PROFESSIONALIZATION OF NURSING IN THE 1890'S. Vogel, Morris J. and Rosenberg, Charles E., ed. *The Therapeutic Revolution: Essays in the Social History of American Medicine (Philadelphia: U. of Pennsylvania Pr., 1979): 201-244.*

In 1889, Jane Addams founded Hull House in Chicago and Isabel Hampton became director of the new nursing school in Baltimore, the Johns Hopkins Hospital Training School for Nurses. These two women revolutionized social welfare and health care in the late 19th century. With the support of founder

Johns Hopkins and the president of the board of trustees, Francis T. King, Hampton strove to professionalize nursing, then characterized by low pay, low status, long hours, and heavy work by working class women. Johns Hopkins, as well as other nursing institutions in the United States, based their reforms on Florence Nightingale's work at St. Thomas's Hospital's nursing school founded in London in 1860. Hampton continued working from the sidelines until her death in 1910.

ROOSEVELT, ELEANOR

213. Lash, Joseph P. ELEANOR ROOSEVELT'S ROLE IN WOMEN'S HISTORY.
Deutrich, Mabel E. and Purdy, Virginia C., ed.
Clio Was a Woman: Studies in the History of American Women (Washington, D.C.: Howard U. Pr., 1980): 243-253.

Recounts Eleanor Roosevelt's career. Raised by a grandmother who was the epitome of Victorian female dependence and helplessness, Mrs. Roosevelt did not have a childhood upbringing which nurtured traits of independence and militancy. She was influenced in her conception of how women should participate in political life by her aunt, Mrs. Cowles, emerging as a champion of women's rights. She was also influenced to become more of a public person by the US entry into World War I and by the discovery of her husband's romance with Lucy Mercer. During the 1920's she became a leader in her own right with active participation in many organizations. The New Deal years represented a high point in women's participation in politics and government, largely because of Mrs. Roosevelt. A discussion summary follows.Royden, Agnes Maude

214. Downing, Arthur. POLITICAL CHRISTIANITY IN ACTION: THE CRUSADES OF AGNES MAUDE ROYDEN.
J. of the Rutgers U. Lib. 1984 46(1): 28-38.

Although her name is unfamiliar today, less than 50 years ago Agnes Maude Royden was renowned both in the United States and Great Britain as a social reformer. Her concerns included such volatile issues as disarmament, women's suffrage, labor organization, venereal disease, independence for Ireland, the rights of prostitutes, and women in the clergy. For Royden, the remedy for social ills was political action; she intertwined politics, religion, and social reform.

S

SABIN, ELLEN B.

215. Pau On Lau, Estelle. ELLEN B. SABIN: PIONEER EDUCATOR. *Pacific Hist. 1978 22(2): 145-160.*

Ellen B. Sabin contributed to the development of teaching and the education of women. She simultaneously attended the University of Wisconsin and taught school during 1866-68. She moved with her family to Oregon in 1872 and continued her innovative teaching techniques in the Portland schools. In 1874 she became principal of the Old North School in Portland, where she had two problems: discipline and dirt. Visiting homes of her pupils, she imparted instruction to the family and showed mothers how to keep homes clean. Appointed head of Downer College in 1890 and Milwaukee Downer College in 1895, she guided the consolidated institutions, expanded their curriculum, and championed their commitment to educate women for their role in society.

SACAGAWEA

216. Schroer, Blanche. BOAT-PUSHER OR BIRD WOMAN? SACAGAWEA OR SACAJAWEA? *Ann. of Wyoming 1980 52(1): 46-54.*

Investigates the debate inaugurated by Grace Raymond Hebard during the 1920's and 1930's that an Indian woman named Porivo was the original Sacagawea who had accompanied the 1804-06 Lewis and Clark Expedition. Evidence indicates that Porivo, who died on Wyoming's Wind River Reservation in 1884, was not Sacagawea, although she may have encountered the original Sacagawea (who died in 1812) or heard stories of her exploits. Anna Lee Waldo's *Sacajawea* (New York: Avon, 1979) adopts the improbable Porivo theme and creates an even more improbable story loosely based on Porivo's life.

SANDOZ, MARI

217. Bancroft, Caroline. TWO WOMEN WRITERS: CAROLINE BANCROFT RECALLS HER DAYS WITH MARI SANDOZ. *Colorado Heritage 1982 (1): 103-111.*

Provides a brief biography of Mari Sandoz prior to 1940, when she moved to Denver "to concentrate on research for a biography of Crazy Horse." Sandoz and the author became close friends. Both were interested in 19th-century Far West history, politics, poetry, art, people, horses, wildflowers, and psychic phenomena. Sandoz was a generous, versatile, courageous, and independent person who denied all religion, for a time admired Communism, and had a great affinity for the Indians. Work was her passion. She wrote numerous books, and others were in process when she died of cancer in 1966.

SANFORD, MARIA LOUISE

218. Schofield, Geraldine Bryan and Smith, Susan Margot. MARIA LOUISE SANFORD: MINNESOTA'S HEROINE. Stuhler, Barbara and Kreuter, Gretchen, ed. *Women of Minnesota: Selected Biographical Essays (St. Paul: Minnesota Historical Society Press, 1977): 77-93.*

Maria Louise Sanford, an outstanding teacher, popular lecturer, and civic activist, was born on 19 December 1836 in Old Saybrook, Connecticut. Sanford's formal education ended in 1855 when she graduated from New Britain Normal School. She then taught school and won local fame as a lecturer in Connecticut and Pennsylvania. Her popularity, dynamism, and ideas led Swarthmore College to employ her. In 1880, she became an assistant professor of English at the University of Minnesota. Throughout her career, she attracted large numbers of students, spent long hours in the classroom, maintained a busy schedule as a public speaker, and suffered financial hardships. Her temperament and actions often offended academic colleagues, and she endured many occasions of salary cuts and threatened job dismissals. Despite the academic skirmishes, Sanford retained the loyalty and support of many former students, civic organizations, and public figures. When she retired, in 1909, Sanford was a respected and prominent

Minnesota resident. She continued to lead a busy life and worked as a public speaker and fund raiser for women's clubs, black churches and schools, child labor reform, and prohibition. Her unending speaking engagements took her to all parts of the nation. On 20 April 1920, she gave her last public address, before the national convention of the Daughters of the American Revolution. The next day she died at age 83.

SARGENT, JUDITH SINGER

219. Cederstrom, Eleanor R. "REMEMBER THE LADIES". *Essex Inst. Hist. Collections 1983 119(3): 145-164.*

Examines early feminist Judith Singer Sargent's life, her two marriages, her childbearing experiences, her publications, and her career as a playwright. Sargent, who wrote many essays on the subject of women, penned an essay in 1779 entitled "On the Equality of Sexes," which was not published until 1790 in *Massachusetts Magazine.* Her essays on equality for the sexes argued the need for education as an equalizing device. She should be remembered for her early championing of women and "for her courage in daring to develop her own talents at a time when women were expected to thread a needle rather than wield a pen."

SAVERY, ANNE

220. Noun, Louise. ANNIE SAVERY: A VOICE FOR WOMEN'S RIGHTS.
Ann. of Iowa 1977 44(1): 3-30.

Anne Savery (1831-91), wife of an Iowa hotelkeeper and land developer, struggled for woman suffrage in Iowa. During 1868-72 she and her friend Amelia Bloomer failed to secure a state referendum on the suffrage question. Savery received much blame for the negative vote in the state legislature; it was charged that her refusal to denounce free-love advocate Victoria Woodhull split the suffragist movement and thus ensured its failure.

SCHOFIELD, MARTHA

221. Smedley, Katherine. MARTHA SCHOFIELD AND THE RIGHTS OF WOMEN. *South Carolina Historical Magazine 1984 85(3): 195-210.*

Martha Schofield established and directed the Schofield Normal and Industrial School, for many years one of the foremost schools for blacks in the South, and was a determined political activist and consistent supporter of women's rights. Her first public activity in support of women's rights came in 1871 when she joined the South Carolina branch of the American Woman's Suffrage Association, and she later became known on a national level for playing a role in exposing the success of the South Carolina Democrats in keeping blacks from voting in the election of 1876.

SEDGWICK, CATHARINE MARIA

222. Kelley, Mary. A WOMAN ALONE: CATHARINE MARIA SEDGWICK'S SPINSTERHOOD IN NINETEENTH-CENTURY AMERICA. *New England Q. 1978 51(2): 209-225.*

Catharine Maria Sedgwick (1789-1867) glorified the family and reinforced the belief that women could achieve their greatest fulfillment within the family and make their greatest contribution to society by inculcating values in the family. However, she never married and always sprinkled her works with statements affirming the legitimacy of the unmarried woman's status. Observing the unsatisfactory marriages of friends and relatives she rejected several suitors. Her brothers served as surrogate husbands and their children as her surrogate children. Together they provided her the psychological benefits of a family without the attendant responsibilities.

SHAW, ANNA HOWARD

223. Finn, Barbara R. ANNA HOWARD SHAW AND WOMEN'S WORK. *Frontiers 1979 4(3): 21-25.*

Describes feminist activist Anna Howard Shaw's life from 1865, when, at 18, she became a schoolteacher, until her death in 1919, focusing on the issue of equal opportunity in employment for women which she considered more important than suffrage, and her relationship with Lucy Anthony, niece of Susan B. Anthony, from their meeting in 1888, which lasted 30 years until Shaw's death; 1870's-1919.

SLOSS, HATTIE HECHT

224. Kramer, William M. and Stern, Norton B. HATTIE SLOSS: CULTURAL LEADER AND JEWISH ACTIVIST OF MODERN SAN FRANCISCO. *Western States Jewish Hist. Q. 1982 14(3): 207-215.*

Boston socialite Hattie Hecht married San Francisco attorney Marcus C. Sloss in 1899. She loved her adopted city and became a leader in a broad range of cultural, civic, and religious activities. She helped found the San Francisco Opera Association and the San Francisco Symphony Association. From 1940 to 1955 she broadcast a weekly radio program on classical music. The Bay Cities Associated Charities and the Community Chest were among the organizations she directed. In the Jewish religious community, she was a member of the board of Congregation Emanu-El and founding president of the local Zionist Hadassah.

SMEDLEY, AGNES

225. Duke, David C. SPY SCARES, SCAPEGOATS, AND THE COLD WAR. *South Atlantic Q. 1980 79(3): 245-256.*

Traces the paths of two American women, Agnes Smedley (who died in 1950) and Anna Louise Strong (1885-1970), from the post-World War I period until their respective deaths. Smedley was quite enamored by the Communist movement in China, Strong by the Communist takeover in Russia. Strong was later deported from the USSR for not adhering precisely to the Communist line—a very disenchanting experience for her. Both became scapegoats for Americans and Russians who were looking for excuses for the failures that marked their Cold War ventures.

SMITH, JULIA H.

226. O'Connell, Lucille. JULIA H. SMITH: AN UNCOMMON NEW ENGLANDER. *Phylon 1978 39(3): 275-281.*

Attention to black Americans has been focused largely on the rural South and urban slums, but the black middle classes are not a new phenomenon in this country, and unlike their cousins in the ghettos and on the farms, have maintained a level of achievement and education equal to that of their white neighbors. Julia H. Smith (b. 1885), a Boston aristocrat of Afro-American descent, teacher for a time in the schools of Washington, D. C., community leader in Cambridge, and member of intellectual circles, has never known prejudice first-hand in her long and productive life. Sprung from a family long resident in Boston, distinguished by generations of accomplishment, her life shows what middle-class blacks can do when not exposed to racial discrimination.

SMITH, LILLIAN

227. Gladney, Margaret Rose. LILLIAN SMITH'S HOPE FOR SOUTHERN WOMEN. *Southern Studies 1983 22(3): 274-284.*

Southern writer Lillian Smith saw a relationship between racial and sexual discrimination in Western culture and in Southern women. Society's attitudes toward sexuality and racial segregation were harmful to all society. She published her views in the magazines *Pseudopodia, North Georgia Review*, and *South Today*. According to Smith, if women were only allowed to be wives and mothers—either white ladies or black mammies—they could never be full persons. Men were also hurt and some were led to homosexuality, alcoholism, neuroses, and brutality. Smith established a camp in Laurel Falls, Georgia, where girls discussed themselves and their lives and were led to new insights.

228. Loveland, Anne C. LILLIAN SMITH AND THE PROBLEM OF SEGREGATION IN THE ROOSEVELT ERA. *Southern Studies 1983 22(1): 32-54.*

Lillian Smith, a Southern woman, read and traveled widely in her youth. These experiences led her to reject segregation, and in 1942 she began writing critically of that practice—one of a very few white Southerners who called for an end to racial discrimination. Smith sponsored conferences at which blacks and whites met on equal social grounds; she joined organizations promoting desegregation; and she continued to write extensively. She believed the root of the problem lay in the notion of white superiority, but its damage was the dehumanization of both blacks and whites.

SNOW, ELIZA ROXEY

229. Beecher, Maureen Ursenbach. THE ELIZA ENIGMA. *Dialogue 1978 11(1): 30-43.*

Examines the role of Eliza Roxey Snow (1804-87), plural wife of Joseph Smith and later Brigham Young, in the Mormon Church. Her poetry, begun in her Ohio youth, was important as an expression of her faith but undistinguished as poetry. She spoke in tongues, and was recognized as a prophet by her contemporaries, but most revelations were derivative, and predictions half-fulfilled. She practiced priestly functions in ministering to women in the early church in Utah. Her skills as "presidentess" were those of a succesful administrator rather than an originator.

SPERRY-STEELE, FANNIE

230. Stiffler, Liz and Blake, Tona. FANNIE SPERRY-STEELE: MONTANA'S CHAMPION BRONC RIDER. *Montana 1982 32(2): 44-57.*

Fannie Sperry-Steele rode in the professional rodeo and wild west show circuit from 1907 to 1925. Born on a Montana ranch, Fannie Sperry won the bucking horse contest in 1912 at the Calgary Stampede and became known as Montana's champion bronc rider. In 1913 she married Bill Steele; they toured together until 1925, and from then until 1965 she managed a dude ranch in the Lincoln, Montana area. Discusses the Sperry-Steele family and its professional activities.

STANFORD, JANE LATHROP

231. Nilan, Roxanne. JANE LATHROP STANFORD AND THE DOMESTICATION OF STANFORD UNIVERSITY, 1893-1905. *San Jose Studies 1979 5(1): 7-30.*

Jane Lathrop Stanford, faced with the possibility of financial ruin for Stanford University following the death of Leland Stanford, took charge of financial, administrative, and development matters at the university 1893-1905; from her experience as a mother and housewife, she ran the institution as a household.

STEIN, GERTRUDE

232. Breslin, James E. GERTRUDE STEIN AND THE PROBLEMS OF AUTOBIOGRAPHY. *Georgia Rev. 1979 33(4): 901-913.*

Autobiographical writing posed a challenge for Gertrude Stein (1874-1946), whose desire to live and write in a continuous present logically forced her to reject not only the retrospective mode, but to abjure the notion of identity altogether. *The Autobiography of Alice B. Toklas,* Stein's deceptively-titled reminiscence of her life, reveals an intense and creative struggle with the conventions of memory, identity and chronological time. Emphasizing the surface rather than the psychological core, the autobiography is deliberately stylized and selective, and moves whimsically by free association, liberated from chronological order while still accepting its reality.

STOKES, ROSE PASTOR

233. Renshaw, Patrick. ROSE OF THE WORLD: THE PASTOR-STOKES MARRIAGE AND THE AMERICAN LEFT, 1905-1925. *New York Hist. 1981 62(4): 415-438.*

The story of Rose Pastor and Graham Phelps Stokes, reformers who married in 1905, illustrates the fact that Progressivism and American socialism overlapped at many points and ultimately sought contradictory objectives. Rose, a Russian-Jewish immigrant, and Graham, scion of a wealthy family from New York, joined the Socialist Party by 1906 and were active in the Intercollegiate Socialist Society. During World War I Rose moved further to the left and became an active Communist after the war. After the marriage ended in divorce in 1925, Rose became a less active Communist, while Graham returned to his earlier quest for social reform based on religious principles.

STONE, ELLEN M.

234. Woods, Randall B. TERRORISM IN THE AGE OF ROOSEVELT: THE MISS STONE AFFAIR, 1901-1902. *Am. Q. 1979 31(4): 478-495.*

In September 1901, Ellen M. Stone (1846-1927), an American Congregationalist missionary, was kidnapped and held for ransom by a group of Macedonian nationalists called the Internal Macedonian Revolutionary Organization. During her captivity, the Roosevelt administration, the American public, and Stone's organization, the American Board Commissioners for Foreign Missions, struggled with the issues of international political terrorism. A $66,000 ransom raised by public donations was ultimately accepted by the nationalists, who then freed Stone in February 1902. The ransom helped finance a Macedonian rebellion in August 1903 that was quickly suppressed by the Turks.

STURGEON, SALLIE LEWIS

235. Crockett, Bernice Norman."NO JOB FOR A WOMAN."
Chronicles of Oklahoma 1983 61(2): 148-167.

Sallie Lewis Sturgeon came to Oklahoma in 1894 with her husband, and they soon established residence in Ardmore. There Mrs. Sturgeon became a reporter for the local newspaper and created a weekly "women's news column." She later began publishing *The Oklahoma Lady*, the first exclusively women's journal published in Oklahoma. Despite her own sense of independence in the business world, Mrs. Sturgeon campaigned against women's suffrage. In 1920, Governor J. B. A. Robertson appointed her as the first female member of the Oklahoma State Health Department's team of sanitary inspectors. She diligently carried out her inspector duties and won praise throughout the state.

SUMNER, JEANNIE

236. Curtis, Joy and Curtis, Bruce. ILLNESS AND THE VICTORIAN LADY: THE CASE OF JEANNIE SUMNER.
Int. J. of Women's Studies (Canada) 1981 4(5): 527-543.

Like many late-Victorian middle-class US women, Jeannie Sumner was limited in her potential and development by the rigid sex role prescriptions of her class, to which she responded by becoming a delicate lady whose illnesses prevented her from fulfilling the conflicting duties of both the passive social ornament and the nurturant wife-mother; her life illustrates that the attempt to define role and potential by sex alone damaged not only women, but all of society.

T

TARBELL, IDA M.

237. Stinson, Robert. IDA M. TARBELL AND THE AMBIGUITIES OF FEMINISM.
Pennsylvania Mag. of Hist. and Biog. 1977 101(2): 217-239.

Ida M. Tarbell, an early convert to the suffrage movement, determined not to marry and successfully pursued a journalistic career which reached its peak when she was made managing editor of *McClure's Magazine.* After 1909, her articles and novels about women began to change. She became an advocate of home life and the family, a position she held until her death. Speculations about the reasons for her conversion fail to take into account the fact that she had not really changed but rather was reflecting another side of an ideological bipolarity that had always existed in her mind.

TEASDALE, SARA

238. Drake, William. SARA TEASDALE'S QUIET REBELLION AGAINST THE MIDWEST. *Missouri Hist. Soc. Bulletin 1980 36(4): 221-227.*

St. Louis poet Sara Teasdale (1884-1933) fled from St. Louis and then depended upon European culture and the New York literary milieu for her standards and inspiration. Accordingly, she became a caustic critic of midwestern life and culture. For that reason, she spurned the 1913-14 courtship of author Vachel Lindsay (1879-1931) whom she considered a representative of the "literary Midwest."

TELLES, LUCY

239. Bates, Craig D. LUCY TELLES: AN OUTSTANDING WEAVER OF THE MIWOK-PAIUTE. *Pacific Hist. 1980 24(4): 396-430.*

The legacy of Lucy Telles (ca. 1870-1956), a Miwok-Paiute Indian weaver, to the world of American Indian art is significant. She developed a new style of basketry, using traditional techniques and materials blended with new designs and forms to create a unique aesthetic experience. She blended the best of Anglo-Saxon and Indian cultures in her daily life and was able to create a harmonious blending of the old and new in her weaving. Her efforts resulted not only in winning many prizes but also in the creation of a basketry style that belongs uniquely to one people of one place and time.

V

VALESH, EVA MCDONALD

240. Gilman, Rhoda R. EVA MC DONALD VALESH: MINNESOTA POPULIST. Stuhler, Barbara and Kreuter, Gretchen, ed. *Women of Minnesota: Selected Biographical Essays (St. Paul: Minnesota Historical Society Press, 1977): 55-76.*

During the late 1880's and early 1890's, Eva McDonald Valesh was a leading figure in Minnesota's labor and agrarian political movements. As a journalist and lecturer, Valesh worked for the Knights of Labor, the Farmers' Alliance, and the People's Party. An energetic, ambitious, impassioned lecturer and newspaper reporter, Valesh achieved political power at a time when women's suffrage was not yet seriously discussed even by third parties. She campaigned with Ignatius Donnelly, worked with editor Everett Fish, was elected State Lecturer of the Minnesota Alliance, was a national organizer for the People's Party, and worked for William Jennings Bryan's presidential campaign in 1896. That same year, she and her husband, Frank Valesh, separated. Eva moved with her son to New York City where she worked as a journalist, became involved with the Women's Trade Union League, and wed wealthy Benjamin F. Cross. After this marriage ended, Eva resumed work as a proofreader and worked for the *New York Times* until she retired, in 1951, at age 85. When she died five years later, people had long since forgotten her years of political activism in Minnesota.

W

WALKER, LUCY

241. Tomes, Nancy. "LITTLE WORLD OF OUR OWN": THE PENNSYLVANIA HOSPITAL TRAINING SCHOOL FOR NURSES, 1895-1907. *J. of the Hist. of Medicine and Allied Sci. 1978 33(4): 507-530.*

Lucy Walker was superintendent of the Pennsylvania Hospital Training School for Nurses in Philadelphia from 1895 to 1907. She improved discipline and improved the quality of nursing care. She established a strict hierarchical system, and insisted on absolute discipline from her students. By 1899 she had replaced the untrained nurses at the hospital with her own graduates. Most of the students were from small towns, and they were Protestant. They had a wide range of educational background. For those who were educated, nursing was a respectable alternative to medical school. For others, it was a livelihood rather than a profession. The school did not attract or accept urban working class women. One problem was class conflict between the middle class students and the working class patients. Lucy Walker sought to improve the nursing profession. She transmitted to American hospitals British methods which were the beginning of professionalization. American nurses followed her in adapting those forms to the 20th-century hospital.

SUBJECT INDEX

Each biographical summary in this book is indexed below with a group (or "string") of index terms. Each of the terms in these strings will move around to the first or leading position in the string so that the entire index string will appear in the subject index as many times as there are terms in the string. This way, there are several different ways to access each biographical summary.

Each of the index strings appears in alphabetical order according to the leading term in bold. If a leading term is exactly the same as the leading term of the string preceding it, then it is replaced by a dash.

The final term in the string is a number in italics; this number refers to the number of the entry, not the page number on which the entry appears. The dates that precede the italicized entry number are the dates of the time period covered by the biographical article.

A

Abolition Movement. Authors. Children. Feminism. 1820-80. *86*

Acculturation. Educators. Indian-White Relations. Oklahoma. Seminole Indians. 1870-1935. *106*

Actors and Actresses. Bean, Roy. Frontier and Pioneer Life. Great Britain. Western States. ca 1880-1904. *172*

—. Morality. Sex Symbols. 1915-19. *21*

Adams, John. Domesticity. Massachusetts. 1774-82. *2*

Advice column. Feminism. Louisiana. New Orleans *Picayune* (newspaper). 1895-1900. *147*

Air Forces. World War II. 1919-42. *134*

Alaska. Gold Rushes. Klondike Stampede. Monuments. Pack animals. White Pass Trail. Yukon Territory. 1898-1929. *157*

—. Gold Rushes. Personal narratives. 1890's-1918. *181*

—. Mask-makers. Sculptors. 1971-82. *73*

Alaska (Cape Prince of Wales). Lopp, W. T. "Tom". Missions and Missionaries. 1892-1902. *176*

Alaska (Sinuk River). Eskimos. Reindeer. 1890-1907. *18*

Alaska (Sitka). Attitudes. Frontier and Pioneer Life. Letters. Teaching. 1888. *109*

—. California. Photographers, naturalistic. Southwest. 1899-1963. *19*

—. Comic strips. Cooney family (reminiscences). Illustration. Montana (Canyon Ferry). 1896-1972. *97*

—. Illinois (Springfield). Natural History. 1931-66. *127*

Artists. Idaho (Boise). 1847-92. *133*

Assimilation. California (Chico). Maidu Indians. 1868-1918. *40*

Athletes. Boosterism. New Jersey (Paterson). Track and field. 1909-32. **125**

Attitudes. Alaska (Sitka). Frontier and Pioneer Life. Letters. Teaching. 1888. *109*

—. Art. Massachusetts. 1810-50. *142*

—. Courtship. Lindsay, Vachel. North Central States. Poetry. 1913-14. *238*

—. Domesticity. 1830-80. *175*

Authors. Abolition Movement. Children. Feminism. 1820-80. *86*

—. Alcott, Amos Bronson. Family. Social Change. Theater. 1832-88. *9*

—. American Revolution. Massachusetts. 1740-1814. *242*

—. Bancroft, Caroline. Personal narratives. 1941-66. *217*

—. Blacks. Desegregation. Race Relations. South. Whites. 1940-50. *228*

—. California. Feminism. Nationalist movement. Socialism. 1888-95. *146*

—. Civil Rights. Indians, Sioux (Yankton). National Council of American Indians. 1900-38. *47*

—. Cleyrergue, Berthe (interview). France (Paris). Salons. 1909-72. *22*

—. Davis, Jefferson. Mississippi. 1889-1906. *107*

—. Editors. Lane, Rose Wilder. 1903-32. *245*

—. Feminists. 1770-1800. *219*

—. Feminists. Novelists. 1890's-1910's. *20*

—. Racism. Sex Discrimination. Social Reform. South. 1940-50. *227*

—. South Carolina (Charleston). 1826-87. *83*

—. Western States. 1890's-1940's. *80*

Autobiography. 1874-1946. *232*

B

Bancroft, Caroline. Authors. Personal narratives. 1941-66. *217*

Baptists. Minnesota (St. Paul). Social reformers. 1847-83. *41*

—. Missions and Missionaries. Oklahoma (Wichita

C

Domesticity. Adams, John. Massachusetts. 1774-82. *2*

—. Attitudes. 1830-80. *175*

—. Middle Classes. 1797-1812. *4*

Douglas, Stephen A. (statue). Governor's mansion. Illinois. Personal Narratives. Sculpture. 1850's-65. *117*

Downtown Community School. New York City. Progressive education. School Integration. 1928-76. *185*

Dramatists. Blacks. Composers. 1930-50. *149*

E_____

Editors. Authors. Lane, Rose Wilder. 1903-32. *245*

—. Canada. Librarians. 1926-78. *190*

—. *Home Monthly.* 1896-1900. *77*

—. Mormons. Utah. ca 1869-1944. *209*

Education. 1899-1973. *196*

—. Blacks. North Carolina (Greensboro). Palmer Memorial Institute. 1902-61. *67*

—. Delaware (Brandywine region). 1800-17. *119*

—. Kentucky (Lexington). Private Schools. 1790's-1833. *29*

—. Minnesota. 1883-1972. *173*

—. Montana. 1883-1952. *100*

—. Philanthropists. 1862-1919. *158*

Educational Administrators. California. Stanford University. 1893-1905. *231*

Educational philosophers. Blacks. Institute for Colored Youth. Pennsylvania (Philadelphia). 1865-1913. *96*

Educational Reformers. Jews. New York City. Social Reformers. 1880-1912. *210*

Educators. 19c-20c. *30*

—. Acculturation. Indian-White Relations. Oklahoma. Seminole Indians. 1870-1935. *106*

—. Blacks. Civil Rights. Schofield Normal and Industrial School. South Carolina. Suffrage. 1860's-1908. *221*

—. Blacks. Episcopal Church, Protestant. 1875-1981. *12*

—. Iowa. Rural Schools. 1905-40. *192*

—. Nevada, University of. Woman Suffrage. 1824-1908. *89*

Elites. South Carolina. 1850's-99. *204*

Emerson, Ralph Waldo. District of Columbia. Journalists. 1850-96. *115*

Employment. Anthony, Lucy. Equal opportunity. Feminism. 1865-1919. *223*

—. New Deal. 1933-38. *249*

G

H

—. Charity of Providence, Sisters of. Construction. Pacific Northwest. 1856-1902. *179*

Poetry. Attitudes. Courtship. Lindsay, Vachel. North Central States. 1913-14. *238*

—. California (San Francisco). 1850's-80's. *95*

—. Massachusetts (Amherst). 1847-86. *111*

Poets. Davidson, Margaret Miller. Death and Dying. 1810-50. *105*

Police. Ontario (Toronto). Social problems. 1900-34. *200*

Political activism. Journalism. Lectures. Minnesota. Populism. 1866-1956. *240*

Political Advocates. Kansas. Populists. 1871-1933. *174*

Political Leaders. Diaries. Mormons. Social Reformers. Utah. 1897-1967. *191*

Political Leadership. Community organizations. Race Relations. Texas, east. 1930's-70's. *113*

Political Participation. New Deal. 1900-36. *213*

Political Protest. Folk Songs. Labor Unions and Organizations. Red Dust Players (troupe). Theater. 1930's. *104*

Politics. Armies. Trans-Mississippi West. 1841-1902. *138*

—. Georgia. Senate. Woman suffrage. 1860's-1922. *131*

—. Great Britain. Religion. Social reform. 1900-50. *214*

—. Literature. Peace. Racism. 1950's-65. *155*

—. Nevada Historical Society. Public Finance. Scrugham, James. 1920's. *244*

Polygamy. Great Britain. Letters. Mormons. Utah (Salt Lake City). 1885-96. *72*

Populism. Journalism. Lectures. Minnesota. Political activism. 1866-1956. *240*

Populists. Kansas. Political Advocates. 1871-1933. *174*

Porivo. Hebard, Grace Raymond. Historiography. Lewis and Clark Expedition. Waldo, Anna Lee. 1804-1980. *216*

Presbyterian Church. Missions and Missionaries. New Mexico (Trementina). 1910-50. *44*

—. Sunday Schools. 1800-50. *35*

Presbyterian Mission Home. California (San Francisco). Chinese Americans. Missions and Missionaries. 1869-1920. *71*

Prisoners of War. Diaries. Philippines. World War II. 1941-44. *103*

Private Schools. Education. Kentucky (Lexington). 1790's-1833. *29*

Professionalization. Frontier Nursing Service. Kentucky. Medical care. Midwives.

—. Geneva Political Equality Club. New York, western. Suffrage. 1897-1912. *187*

—. Libraries (public). Minnesota (Minneapolis). Women. 1890's-1953. *99*

—. Social work. 1904-54. *145*

—. Socialist Party. 1905-25. *233*

Reindeer. Alaska (Sinuk River). Eskimos. 1890-1907. *18*

Religion. Friendship. Mount Holyoke College. 1848-50. *110*

—. Great Britain. Politics. Social reform. 1900-50. *214*

—. Literature. Massachusetts Bay Colony. Social change. 1630's-70's. *55*

Reporters. Columnists. Oklahoma. 1908-61. *167*

—. Federal Emergency Relief Administration. Hopkins, Harry. Iowa. Minnesota. 1933. *159*

Revolutionary Movements. Immigrants. Liberal Party. Mexico. Personal narratives. Texas (El Paso). 1890-1911. *16*

Rodeos. Montana (Lincoln). 1887-1965. *230*

Roosevelt, Theodore (administration). American Board Commissioners for Foreign Missions. Internal Macedonian Revolutionary Organization. Kidnapping. Macedonia. Missions and

Missionaries. Terrorism. 1901-02. *234*

Rural areas. Frontier Nursing Service. Kentucky. Medical care. Midwives. Nurses and Nursing. Professionalization. 1925-37. *59*

Rural life. Depressions. Idaho (Pocatello area). Personal narratives. 1931-40. *139*

—. Diaries. Farms. Ohio (Fayette County). 1836-45. *6*

—. Illinois. Personal narratives. Teachers. 1851-1927. *66*

Rural Schools. Educators. Iowa. 1905-40. *192*

S

St. Teresa, College of. Catholic Church. Franciscan Sisters. Minnesota (Winona). 1903-54. *189*

Salons. Authors. Cleyrergue, Berthe (interview). France (Paris). 1909-72. *22*

Sanitary inspectors. Journalism. Oklahoma. 1894-1930's. *235*

Saskatchewan. Alberta (Red Deer River area). Homesteaders. Missionaries. Personal narratives. 1905-64. *68*

Savoy Theatre. Films. Oklahoma (Prague). 1921-58. *188*

Schofield Normal and Industrial School. Blacks. Civil Rights. Educators. South

—. Letters. Mormons. 1837-69.
38

—. Mormons. 1840-50. *39*

Social Change. Alcott, Amos
Bronson. Authors. Family.
Theater. 1832-88. *9*

—. Literature. Massachusetts
Bay Colony. Religion. 1630's-
70's. *55*

Social customs. Courtship.
Letters. 1839-43. *43*

Social problems. Ontario
(Toronto). Police. 1900-34.
200

Social Reform. Authors.
Racism. Sex Discrimination.
South. 1940-50. *227*

—. Great Britain. Politics.
Religion. 1900-50. *214*

—. New Jersey (Jersey City).
Public Welfare. Settlement
houses. Whittier House. 1890-
1935. *53*

Social reformers. 1880-1920. *7*

—. Baptists. Minnesota (St.
Paul). 1847-83. *41*

—. Diaries. Mormons. Political
Leaders. Utah. 1897-1967.
191

—. Educational Reformers.
Jews. New York City. 1880-
1912. *210*

—. Feminists. Suffrage.
Tennessee. 1860's-1917. *186*

—. Washington (Seattle area).
1880's-1902. *201*

—. Youth. 1860-89. *8*

Social status. Iowa. Self-image.
1850-1900. *5*

Social Work. Illinois (Chicago).
Johns Hopkins Hospital
Training School for Nurses.
Maryland (Baltimore). Nurses
and Nursing.
Professionalization. 1889-
1910. *212*

—. Reform. 1904-54. *145*

Social Workers. Christians.
Hull House. 1885-1900. *153*

—. Women's Christian
Temperance Union. ca 1855-
1900. *247*

Socialism. Authors. California.
Feminism. Nationalist
movement. 1888-95. *146*

Socialist Party. Reform. 1905-
25. *233*

South. Authors. Blacks.
Desegregation. Race Relations.
Whites. 1940-50. *228*

—. Authors. Racism. Sex
Discrimination. Social Reform.
1940-50. *227*

—. Diaries. Slavery. 19c. *84*

South Carolina. Blacks. Civil
Rights. Educators. Schofield
Normal and Industrial School.
Suffrage. 1860's-1908. **221**

—. Elites. 1850's-99. *204*

South Carolina (Charleston).
Authors. 1826-87. *83*

**South Carolina (Spartanburg
District).** Civil War. Daily
life. Diaries. Farmers. 1861-
65. *156*

—. Canada. China. Missions
and Missionaries. Personal
narratives. Teaching. 1928-45.
161

—. Diaries. Philippines.
Prisoners of War. 1941-44.
103

**World's Columbian Exposition
(Chicago, 1893).** North
Carolina. 1890-95. *98*

Y_____

Young, Brigham. Illinois
(Nauvoo). Mormons. Smith,
Joseph. 1832-79. *37*

Youth. Social reformers. 1860-
89. *8*

Yukon Territory. Alaska. Gold
Rushes. Klondike Stampede.
Monuments. Pack animals.
White Pass Trail. 1898-1929.
157

AUTHOR INDEX

LIST OF PERIODICALS

Agricultural History

Alaska Journal

Alberta History

American Heritage

American History Illustrated

American Indian Quarterly

American Jewish History

American Quarterly

American West

Annals of Iowa

Annals of Wyoming

Arizona and the West (now Journal of the Southwest)

Atlantis

Beaver

Biography

Brigham Young University Studies

Bulletin of the History of Medicine

California Historical Quarterly

California History

Canadian Library Journal

Canadian Review of American Studies

Chronicles of Oklahoma

Civil War History

Civil War Times Illustrated

Colorado Heritage

Colorado Magazine

Crisis

Daughters of the American Revolution Magazine

Delaware History

Dialogue

Essex Institute Historical Collections

Feminist Studies

Foundations

Frontiers

Gateway Heritage

Georgia Life

Georgia Review

Great Plains Quarterly

Hayes Historical Journal

Historian

Historical Magazine of the Protestant Episcopal Church

History of Education Quarterly

Horizon

Idaho Yesterdays

Indiana Magazine of History

International Journal of Women's Studies

International Social Science Review

Journal of American Folklore

Journal of American Studies

Journal of Ethnic Studies

Journal of Family History

Journal of Forest History

Journal of Long Island History

Journal of Mississippi History

Journal of Negro Education

Journal of Presbyterian History

Journal of Psychohistory

Journal of the Canadian Church Historical Society

Journal of the History of Medicine and Allied Sciences

Journal of the History of the Behavioral Sciences

Journal of the Illinois State Historical Society (now Illinois Historical Journal)

Journal of the Rutgers University Libraries

Journal of the West

Kansas History

Lituanus

Louisiana History

Maryland Historical Magazine

Massachusetts Review

Masterkey

Mid-America

Midwest Quarterly

Minnesota History

Missouri Historical Review

Missouri Historical Society Bulletin
(superseded by Gateway Heritage)

Montana

Negro History Bulletin

Nevada Historical Society Quarterly

New England Historical and
Genealogical Register

New England Quarterly

New Jersey History

New York History

North Carolina Historical Review

North Louisiana Historical Association
Journal

Ohio History

Old Northwest

Oregon Historical Quarterly

Pacific Historian

Pacific Northwest Quarterly

Pennsylvania Magazine of History and
Biography

Phylon

Proceedings of the South Carolina
Historical Association

Prologue

Psychohistory Review

Radical America

Register of the Kentucky Historical
Society

Rendezvous

San Jose Studies

Signs

Smithsonian

South Atlantic Quarterly

South Carolina Historical Magazine

South Dakota Historical Collections

South Dakota History

Southern Exposure

Southern Studies

Studies in the American Renaissance

Supreme Court Historical Society
Yearbook

Swedish Pioneer Historical Quarterly

Tennessee Historical Quarterly

Utah Historical Quarterly

Vermont History

Vitae Scholasticae

Western States Jewish Historical
Quarterly

Women's Studies